U.S.N.A.:
The United States
of North America

Gordon F. Jones

U.S.N.A.:
The United States of
North America

EP

Erser & Pond

Editor: Norma Harper
Cover design: Benjamin Beaumont
Cover photo: bubaone

Published by Erser & Pond Publishers, Ltd.
1096 Queen St., Suite 225, Halifax, N.S., Canada B3H 2R9

Library and Archives Canada Cataloguing in Publication

Jones, Gordon F., 1930-
    U.S.N.A. /Gordon F. Jones.

ISBN 978-0-9865683-6-7

    1. Canada--Annexation to the United States. 2. Canada--Foreign relations--United States. 3. United States--Foreign relations--Canada. I. Title.

FC249.J653 2012   327.71073   C2012-900817-6

TABLE OF CONTENTS

I dedicate this book to
all the Americans who,
like my dogs,
never really understood
why they had to be impounded
when they crossed the Canadian border.

*We do not learn much from academic tomes,
but from true, sincere, human books,
full of frank and honest thoughts.*

— Henry David Thoreau (attributed)

FOREWORD

What and where in the world is the USNA? No, it isn't the United States Naval Academy. Well it is, but that's not the USNA I have in mind. The one I mean doesn't exist yet. In my mind the acronym USNA stands for the United States of North America. An acronym is sort of like a nickname – it's a shortened way to identify the name of a large and complex organization such as NATO or OPEC. To create an acronym for a very large governmental organization that doesn't exist is perhaps excessively optimistic on my part. Nevertheless, in writing on this subject I'm going to use USNA to connote a proposal that involves the unification of Canada and the United States into a single continental entity.

My qualifications for making this unsolicited proposal are few, and they don't come with any group or individual stamp of approval. But I am a dual citizen, and I have lived approximately half my life in each country. I'm intensely interested in the welfare of both countries, and a life-long history buff. Although I'm eighty-two years old and ought to know better, I still remain an optimist. I perceive a synergy of benefits from a union of my two nationalities, the like of which has never occurred peacefully on this troubled planet. Harboring great hope and no illusions about the difficulties involved, I have decided to write down my thoughts on the subject. I confess that I'm very much in favor (or favour) of the concept of joining the two nations.

After a confession like that, the reader may wish to chuck this little book in the trash without further ado. I would prefer it if he or she were to read it first, but I do realize that we don't always get what we want in this life. I can make no claim to having worked out every single detail, or even most of the particulars that would be involved in such a merger, but there are many thousands of lawyers and politicians in both Canada and the United States who are currently working on much less interesting projects. There is no doubt that they could tend to the specifics if they were challenged to do so. Be forewarned, however, that the naysayers will come out of the woodwork in their thousands, spouting words like impossible, too complex, naïve. My only purpose in writing this book is to get citizens of both countries to see the incredible opportunities that would accrue from a merger of their nations. If I can't make the case for USNA well enough for you to accept it, then you may reject it, but at least you will have heard the pro side of the debate.

Gordon F. Jones
Citizen (Canada & USA)

The total area of Canada is 9,984,670 square kilometers. Of this area 9,093,507 km² is land, and 891,163 km² is fresh water. The total area of the U.S.A. is 9,629,090 km². Of this area, 9,629,090 km² is land and 470,131 km² is fresh water.

CHAPTER ONE

Overlapping History

Motivation is unfortunately nearly always selfish. It is forever self-interested, and either individually or collectively opportunistic. Because most people are disposed to take advantage of situations that will benefit them or their families, friends, neighbors, tribes, or nations, their actions tend to be predicated on what they perceive to be best for themselves. We can safely assume that the motives of Spain, England, France, Portugal, and the Netherlands in the 15th , 16th, and 17th centuries were no holier, selfless, or more magnanimous than was usual for their time. Their motives in regard to the New World displayed opportunistic greed toward the unsuspecting first inhabitants that happened to reside in America. The royal houses in Europe also evinced murderous, warlike competitiveness toward one another. In such an international environment there was nothing for it but to grab what you could and hold on tight. Reacting to the disdainful, arms-length authority of their royal masters, the colonists had little choice but to realize that they were only pawns in a European power game, and as a result they went down the road to independence in the best way they could.

Historians have done a good job of documenting the details of how the formation of the colonies occurred. It's not my intention to go over specific portions of the story, but rather to sum up the motivations of the mother countries as well as the aspirations of their pioneering children in the new land. My conclusion is that the main motivation for both parties was enrichment. The kings sought to take advantage of the easy pickings to be found in the West. Whether it was gold for the Spaniards, furs for the French, land for the Dutch, or fish and trade for Britain, the motive was always the same – the selfish pursuit of easily obtained wealth.

The settlers' motives were only a little better. They, too, were out to get rich, but at least they were willing to work for it. Theirs was not solely an organized venture into legalized, large-scale brigandage. In the early years the colonists were adventurers, loyal to the crowns which had sponsored their voyages. Later immigrants wanted to escape the religious persecution of kings and churches acting in concert to control their personal freedom as individuals.

Operating just beneath these spoken moral objectives, however, was their sub-rosa goal of becoming rich in the New World. Acquiring land, free to those who would work it, was an opportunity that most agricultural workers in Europe found hard to resist. In Europe they toiled for the lairds, aristocrats and gentry without the hope of ever owning their own land. Trades-people likewise enjoyed the prospect of starting and owning their own businesses in a free society. Naturally they grouped themselves into various bastions of people whose ethnicity, religion, language, or loyalty glued them together in community. More importantly they acted in concert with others whose principal motivations they shared, regardless of their place in society or their country of origin.

These enclaves had little experience with self-government. They relied on the same governing systems that they knew, but naturally these came into conflict in the New World as they did in the old. The familiar heritage of English, French and Spanish cultures was parachuted into America where they overlapped and clashed. Questions of loyalty were brought to the fore, until finally fidelity to their nations of origin assumed a lesser role to the opportunities for financial enrichment. This objective was at the root of the true motivations of all the colonists. Unfortunately the relatively petty ethnic, national, and religious loyalties blinded many for a long time to their real purpose in coming to America.

Divisions were created in the New World that hung on from a Europe that was increasingly irrelevant to the situation in America. During the period when the various ethnicities were sorting themselves out, many artificial divisions were created that have had a lasting effect on the unity of the people in the newly-discovered American continent. The nation that was being formed beneath the rivalries on the surface had a binding effect that was stronger than the trivial separations of narrower foreign interests. The United Empire Loyalists, those colonists who fought the American revolutionaries in order to remain loyal to England, were sent to the Maritime Provinces of Canada when the Americans won their independence. These loyalties, and others like them, impeded the progress of a unified new continent. Colonists who placed their original loyalties ahead of unification delayed the inevitable rational continental merger. The forming of a national identity in combination with a majority of their fellow citizens was for a long time regarded as unnecessary.

But after nearly three hundred years of government from afar, the colonial people yearned to govern themselves, control their own affairs, and remove themselves from foreign political intrigues. They wished to avoid taxation without representation and other policies that were being enforced by their countries of origin and levied upon them in order to pay for European political crises not of their making.

Of course by this time they had set up local methods of governance, but these weren't satisfactory to handle national matters of diplomacy, war, and citizen rights. The colonists ached for independence from their European masters, who were profiting immensely from their efforts. It mattered little if Spain, France or England controlled them — the point was

that the absentee landlords in Europe were squeezing the
blood out of their colonial tenants. Without consideration for
their colonists, the mother countries were constantly drawing
them into their wars. These pioneers were worse off than
indentured servants because there was no term limit to their
service. In hindsight it is perfectly clear that the colonists had
to rebel. The ideas of personal and religious freedom that
underpinned the events that led to the American Revolution
and the formation of the Republic were the first of their type.
The French Revolution followed, and its causes partially
overlapped and were inspired by the one in America.

The bloody abuses of the French Revolution brought on
the backlash that resulted in Napoleon's take-over of France
and his attempted conquest of Europe. The Emperor needed
cash to fund his military operations in Europe, and he needed
it fast. Spain was about to cede New Orleans to the French as
a sop to Napoleon for peace at home. It was at this time that
President Thomas Jefferson, in one of those incidents when
one man changed the course of history, arranged the Louisiana
Purchase. The 15 million dollars he paid for the land doubled
the area of the United States, bringing it to the size of Europe.
It was the largest and best land bargain up to that date in the
history of the world. Though everyone now recognizes the
Louisiana Purchase as the deal of the century, Jefferson knew
that making the acquisition was beyond his constitutional
powers. He received much opposition for it at the time, but he
managed to get the approval of Congress, and in so doing a
precedent was set that opens the way for future mergers in
North America.

Overlapping minor motives have conspired all along to
confuse, divide, conceal and segregate the populations in
North America. The larger, more important aspirations of the
immigrant peoples of Canada and the U.S. are uniform, but the
similarity has been kept in a state of denial throughout their
young histories. The reasons for the existence of Canada and

the United States as separate nations are feeble, and anathema to the real ambitions of their peoples today. It should be clear to anyone with an open mind that it was a travesty of major proportions to have allowed North America to be sliced up by imperialist, warring European nations whose only interest was to milk the newly-discovered American cow for all it was worth. The only thing that would be worse for the people of North America would be to allow this fiasco to continue.

What is the truth about our mutual continental ambitions? Why have exclusionary political policies kept our peoples separate? These are the underlying historical issues that must be examined with an open mind as we consider what brought us to our present state, and what we can do to secure the future prosperity of Canada and the United States. Coming to terms with this issue will require that we take a very hard look at ourselves. We will have to see beyond the emotional appeal of misplaced patriotism and consider issues of broader significance to our continent and the world's future.

This kind of big picture thinking is not everyone's cup of tea. Large changes in principles long held to be sacrosanct are not easy to shuck off. If we reduce our motives to the least common denominator we will see that the adage, "it's not the money, it's the principle" is wrong. It's the money, not the principle. The immigrants of today seem to have no trouble in grasping this fact. People come from every part of the world to enjoy prosperity in Canada and the U.S. The fact that the U.S. dollar has effectively become the legal tender of the world is a tribute to the fact that money makes the world go around.

I hardly dare to suggest that money is more important to people than principles lest I appear desperately cynical, but I've found that many people will disregard their principles for the right price. The price may not always be cash; it could also be the threat of physical harm to self or loved ones. Whatever the situation, people have learned that ideals can quite easily be set aside by deals made when life hangs in the balance. Famous and ordinary people alike have forsaken their national loyalty or family ties in order to stay alive. We have to learn to deal with it. If we can recognize that our people are not so different in moral substance than those in other parts of the world, perhaps we can take our future into our own hands. Let us suppose that everyone in the world is out to take care of number one. Let's also suppose that we can ignore the outcries of protests to the contrary and just concentrate on making every citizen wealthy so we can get that out of the way too. What would be the best way to do it?

History indicates that we should generate a prevailing mood of optimism in which to operate. People get wealthy when the economy booms. That may sound too obvious to merit attention, but bear with me. What we want to know is why do the booms occur? The really big ones occur because of some massive "Black Swan" event that unpredictably affect the economy. Sometimes it's caused by a discovery such as those that the explorers and pioneers turned up in America. Fish, furs, fertile land, ore deposits, coal, and oil all made significant contributions to a booming economy in their time and place. Later inventions and innovations made in the industrial sector were another cause of economic booms. Automobiles, planes, and telecommunications have all made their contributions to the boom cycles.

But perhaps the biggest contributor to the various boom cycles has been political. The acquisition of the land in the Louisiana Purchase from France, the Texas land gained from Mexico, Florida from Spain, and Alaska from Russia — all have tremendously boosted local and national treasuries and enriched millions of people.

So what should we do now to give our two economies the next shot of energy that we sorely need? Read on.

CHAPTER TWO

THE NEW PATRIOTISM

Stephen Decatur, the American naval hero, is quoted as having said, "Our country! In her intercourse with foreign nations may she always be in the right; but our country, *right or wrong.*" John Quincy Adams, known by his peers as "Old Man Eloquent," is quoted to have written in response, "May our country be always successful, but whether successful or otherwise, always right." That's better, but best of all on this topic is this paraphrase of a quote attributed to G.K. Chesterton: "My country right or wrong is the equivalent of saying my mother, drunk or sober." Just as the excessive celebratory nonsense of a self-congratulatory contemporary football player scoring a touchdown is over the top, so too is overweening national pride. Crowds chanting USA, USA will not win us any friends among the other nations of the world. Evidently we don't care, and if we don't care that others see us as arrogant, insensitive, poor sports, then why care if we are also judged to be rich, money-grubbing boors?

If winning the game, defeating others, and profiting from our own efforts are our goals, why aren't we equally up front about our national objectives? We continually hear from our politicians that we should keep our competitive edge in the world. It certainly seems as if our principal national and individual mission is to get constantly wealthier. If this is the case, why don't we just say so and get on with the job? This is not meant to be a criticism, but rather to establish a focal point that we can all concentrate on. Perhaps the United States was created to find the pot of gold at the end of the rainbow and then devise a method of acceptable wealth distribution for its citizens, and eventually all the people of the world. Evidently the U.S. is supposed to lead the world to a similar materialist equality, but one that is the antithesis of communism. Just as wealthy individuals invite imitation by hoi polloi, rich nations invite replication by the poorer ones. We may not entirely approve of it, but prosperity seems to be the bellwether for politicians. If their citizens are becoming wealthier, things are seen to be going well and the government takes the credit, hoping for reelection. In hard times our governors look around for someone to take the blame. Usually this ends up being a competing nation or ideology, and it's off to war we go. Presumably we would like this foolishness to stop, but how do we go about stopping it?

The signs and portents are visible to all. We may want our particular tribe of humans to be the most successful on earth, but we don't want it at the cost of our individual prosperity or the misery of others. Once we humans achieve prosperity we get soft and live in luxury. This invites the less successful neighboring tribes or nations to attack in order to take the wealth. The world is rife with perpetual examples of this, with the fall of the Roman Empire being the most notorious.

Now that the cost of wars is greater than the rewards to be had in victory, we have a different problem. I call it the New Patriotism. It is signified by globalization, and it is embodied by the economies of all the nations of the world. This New Patriotism invites everyone on the planet to share the booty that can be gained by participation in the economic unification process that promises to deliver prosperity to all. Under the New Patriotism people are putting their faith in commercial conquest rather than in military victories. The triumphs in the modern world are, and no doubt will continue to be, gained by the formation of new alliances. These partnerships, following the American model, have delivered wealth through mergers, acquisitions, and international cooperative corporate ventures that are tending to unify the economic systems of the world.

Everything on the planet is now furiously amalgamating itself under the unseen hand of the New Patriotism that is weakening nationalism day by day. Consolidation of one kind or another has been expanding steadily in the attempt to secure prosperity for the citizens of every country. The U.N., NATO, and OPEC, for example, are all symptoms of mankind's wider desire to achieve security and prosperity for everyone and anyone. Whether the objectives are narrow or broad, the people's interests are moving closer together.

The movement may seem imperceptible at times, but over the relatively short spans of a decade or a century, we have seen monumental changes that affect our national loyalties and belief structures. There is no way to stop this movement that is concentrating the societies that man has evolved over time, and perhaps this is the way it was meant to be from the beginning. If so, then my desire to see North America united is only one step in the never-ending state we call progress. My hope is that North American consolidation of economic interests can effectively demonstrate how cooperation can eventually supplant competitiveness as the modus operandi of world politics. In other words, if we can do it, so can the rest of the world.

Every time an immigrant leaves his country of birth to come to North America, he or she is tacitly saying that his chances to improve his situation are more important to him than his love for his native land. Morally it doesn't matter from which country he came. He is now pledging his primary loyalty to the new country and to the economic future he envisions for himself. The patriotic glue that stuck nations together is drying out. People are seeing their new patriotism, with the pursuit of wealth at its core, to be more significant to them in their lives than the romantic notion of national loyalty.

If they were offered a million U.S. dollars to change passports, the vast majority of people in the world would make the change in an instant. Immediately upon earning any money the nouveau riche embark on a program of personal tax avoidance and open off-shore accounts to hide their gains, ill-gotten or otherwise, from their new beneficent nation's government agents. What kind of patriotism is that? Do you think it is any different in Canada than in the U.S.?

It is not an easy decision to leave one's home and family and move to a land of strangers, so the pull has to be exceedingly strong. The centuries that produced long lines of incoming immigrants to North America continue, and the fact that very few immigrants ever permanently return to their countries of origin is proof, however, that they believe that they made the right decision. Besides, where else is there to go? Usually the immigrant must surrender his citizenship in the old country when he takes the oath of citizenship in his new land, so he can't easily go back home.

On the other hand, most countries allow none, or take only miniscule numbers of immigrants into their populations. Only Canada, the United States and Australia still receive large numbers of immigrants, and try to assimilate them without discriminating on the basis of country of origin, race, or religion. Eventually those immigrants that come manipulate the new system so that members of their families can come too. As an example, one elderly Chinese man interviewed on Canadian TV unabashedly said that he had been personally responsible for 95 family members following in his well-worn tracks to British Columbia, Canada.

The movement of peoples to North America has created an overlapping of human aspirations on a scale heretofore unknown, and this has been instrumental in creating the New Patriotism that is sweeping the developing world. Whether we like it or not, the world must adapt itself to the apotheosis of money. Be honest now — would the millions of immigrants who came to America have done so if not to improve their financial situation? We emphasize the freedom aspect of immigration because it makes us feel good to bestow liberty on poor or persecuted people. That is the politically-correct view of our immigration policy, but how many of these immigrants would have come here had it not been for the financial component? Take notice also of the new immigration regulations that offer preferred status to those immigrants who bring money with them when they come. It is presumed that they will use their money to set up businesses and provide jobs for others, and it usually works out that way.

Nowadays we also encourage money to immigrate. This is not a diatribe against governmental immigration policies or the hopes and dreams of immigrants. The new blood has injected energy and talent into the North American economy, and that helps to build our nation. My point is not to criticize anyone, but to understand and admit that the principal motivation for attracting people to our shores now is financial. We must use that fact to continue to enhance life in North America for those already here, as well as for the millions that may yet come. I find no great fault with immigration and those policies that attract immigrants to our land.

I do think, however, that our immigration and naturalization policies should be more transparent, more selective about who is admitted, and better targeted so that we can optimize our growth and strengthen our population's ability to compete in the world. We should consciously and proactively search the world for the most desirable candidates for immigration, and not just wait for immigrant family members or persecuted peoples to apply. North Americans are building a meritocracy, and this requires selectivity. These days every corporation needs a human resources department to select, to hire, and to promote new employees. Governments need this function more than companies do because they are producing new citizens, and they are not easy to get rid of once admitted.

We can't lay off citizens when things get tight.

More than any other single thing, however, we Americans need to exploit our best feature, which is the opportunity to prosper that we give to our human resources. If we understand the forces that are operating in the world today, and squarely face the fact that the New Patriotism is a condition of the wallet and not of the heart, only then can we also improve our national "heart condition."

Look around. Who produces philanthropy? Whether it is individual charity or national benevolence, it is the wealthy who give to the poor, and it will always be that way. The poor and the persecuted are occupied with survival. They can't be expected to improve their philosophical skills until their basic needs are fulfilled. Whether at home or abroad, whether rich or poor, it's nice to have money, and the best way to get it is through commerce. Canada and the United States offer a recipe to a starving world. International trade is the best method of peacefully advancing to the next step in the world's economic and moral development. Peacefully merging Canada and the United States would create an economic powerhouse that would provide the world with an unparalleled example of what freedom and democracy can do.

Obviously a merger of the two countries would entail changes that will be opposed by many individual citizens of both countries. My contention is that the primary objections will be based on relatively unimportant factors that can be countered with facts and logic. Canadians who have ever waited in line at one of the United States borders will have seen an endless procession of trucks flooding from Canada into the U.S. Borders are the pulse points in the economic veins that throb with the blood of North American commerce. Business is the lifeblood flowing back and forth between the two countries, and it provides each nation with a healthy exchange of continuous financial wherewithal. We already are one another's best trading partners. Recognition of free trade resulted in the NAFTA agreement, which has operated with enormous overall profitability for both countries since 1984. However, the principal behind this treaty found its origins decades before with the enactment of the Auto Pact called APTA. It addressed an unfavorable trade balance that had existed for many years to the advantage of the United States. Finding peaceful solutions to trade issues is natural for Canada and the United States, and it is a beacon calling for even more future cooperation.

Except for nationalism, petty local political prejudices, and fear on the part of Canadians that they could be swallowed up, the two countries should and would have been united two hundred years ago between the Revolutionary War and the conclusion of the War of 1812. Since then, a minority of North American settlers, who were too fearful to divorce themselves from British or French hegemony and who were led by a long line of unadventurous prime ministers too afraid to lose their jobs, have tiptoed around the problem of unification for all the subsequent years.

An investor in the stock market doesn't need a magnifying glass to see that most of Canada's largest corporations are already functioning as American subsidiaries. It's difficult to see how calling a company General Motors Canada, Ford Motors Canada, or any of the many other Canadian divisions of U.S. companies makes them Canadian simply by tacking "Canada" onto the end of their names. Was this situation improved by doing the same for Toyota Canada or Honda Canada? It's just as silly when the situation is reversed. The Canada label on the robotic arm of the U.S. Space Shuttle, for example, was built with seldom-mentioned but significant input from American Corporations such as General Dynamics, Rockwell International and IBM. Syncrude Canada, which extracts oil from the Athabasca Oil Sands in Northern Alberta, and with the cooperation of the Sun and Shell Oil Companies, sells most of its production to the United States market. Why don't we stop fooling ourselves into thinking that we are two totally separate entities? Why don't we just merge and be done with all the layers of bureaucracy that only serve to increase the cost of everything. Why are we pretending that we have separate loyalties when we are obviously already joined at the economic hip?

CHAPTER THREE

WE, THE PEOPLE

Are people of any importance to their governments anymore? If we are important, why do we seldom get anything we want from our elected officials? We want prosperity, liberty, and security, but does the general population get any of these from those we have elected to govern us? What we do get are high taxes, nationalism, and a flawed security system largely dependent upon shaky international alliances. What we in Canada and the U.S. are receiving from our governments is the maximum amount of inefficiencies that the citizens can tolerate without rebelling.

Let's examine prosperity first. In the preceding chapter we talked about the fact that people have subtly changed their loyalties over the last couple of decades. The New Patriotism is based upon the system of government and the way the nation can best enrich its citizens. Given the opportunity, people will move anywhere that they feel will improve the odds of accumulating wealth. The population shifts due to immigration give ample proof of this. When the people can't move, they move their money. We've all heard about how the wealthiest people put their money in Swiss banks or offshore accounts. Nearly anyone with investments has at least some money in international companies. The average investor's hope for wealth appreciation lies in diversification. But as a technique, does splitting your bets work? This is a question for the financiers, but it seems to me that it's a tactic designed so as not to lose money, rather than to optimize the chances of making investments grow. It accounts for the great popularity of mutual funds that guarantee a mediocre performance in exchange for loss protection. This is the defensive strategy of those who already have money and don't want to lose it. It is also the strategy of the little guy who doesn't trust the market. Timid politicians employ this method of investing in the future welfare of their people. This is why we have recessions while seldom enjoying progress and prosperity.

How did those who have money get it in the first place? Usually the big money accrues by investing in a long shot, or backing something new. Such an investor goes counter to the security-conscious diversifier and backs the business that he understands best. Inventors like Edison and Bell are of this type, as are the Silicon Valley billionaires. When it comes to success strategies for nations, the same principles apply. The U.S. and Canada made their money by making aggressive financial wagers. Both countries plowed their resources into industries requiring huge capitalization, and were rewarded generously for placing these big bets. Their success became the envy of the world, and people flocked to our shores.

Lately the U.S. and Canada have adopted a defensive strategy in their investment policies for the future. They seem to want to diversify, take few risks, and be satisfied to hold on to what they have. This is not the way our nations were built, and now is not the time to lose our nerve. We hear that big banks and corporations are sitting on huge pots of money, which they refuse to invest because the present risk-averse defensive capital mood has judged the conditions to be unsafe for new investments. As a result of this strategy our economies founder, jobs disappear, and hopes wane. As usual our governments don't lead and don't have original ideas, yet our citizens continue to tolerate them.

We, in North America, have withdrawn our support of the "Manifest Destiny" policy, which aimed to make our continent one unity from coast to coast and from north to south. Instead we have substituted a policy of politically-correct separatism that extols diversity, as if any strong nation were ever built that way. Assimilation is the way our nations will get stronger. Assimilation will provide the impetus for a new economic expansion that would take both countries down the road to prosperity. This would not be a hostile take-over, as many Canadians fear. The U.S. has a history of successful mergers that have been accepted into the federation, creating synergies of great benefit to all. What would Alaska, Texas, Florida, California, and the many states that came from the Louisiana Purchase be like if they had not been part of the prosperity synergy that is the U.S.? By virtue of negotiations, Canada's ten provinces and three territories could easily become new states and enrich their citizens without losing their individuality or their liberty. The provinces of Canada vary one from another as do the states of the Union. The people, the land and the economies of Manitoba, for instance, are closer to those of their bordering states than they are to the Maritime provinces, yet they managed to stay in Canada. Likewise the New England states are analogous to the Maritime provinces, but less like the Midwest. However, I have lived in both countries and I know that the reasons not to assimilate are inferior to those that would see us merge.

Now let's consider the issue of national security. Who would be foolish enough to think that Canada's tiny but very professional military numbering under 100,000, could defend its two huge coastlines as well as the largest border with another country in the world? For many years Canada has depended upon the U.S. military to supply the additional muscle needed to keep Canada free. But free from whom, and under what conditions? The development of Canada as a nation has been a struggle, but it appears that the principal enemy resided within the hearts and minds of its own citizens.

For the first centuries nobody, least of all the brave new settlers or the American Indians, took much notice of those absentee rulers who participated from a distance in exploiting the wealth of the new continent. British and French thrones were too far away and too involved with European rivalries to care about anything other than the sources of revenue found in North America. It was only the avarice of the mother countries that created even a modicum of concern for the far-flung lands of their colonies. Not until there was a chance that they might lose them did the colonial powers have to maintain a military presence of any size.

It was the bloody squabbling among the commercial entities like the Hudson's Bay Company and the Hundred Associates that finally required military intervention by troops of the British and French. The troops on the ground only exacerbated the problems, and skirmishes became battles that became wars. When the continental army emerged victorious in the War of Independence, the Americans began to take charge of the political events in North America. The colonists after the war made the mistake of ignoring those who had been British and French loyalists, and let them go their own way.

Many Canadians feared reprisals from Americans who resented them for siding with England and for using the Indians to help them during the war. They probably were happily surprised that the Americans didn't diligently pursue reprisals. Population at the time was sparse, and landmasses seemingly inexhaustible, so people didn't think much about the long-term future of North American nationalities. This was the point in time when the idea of an independent Canada was born. It would have been far better had it been stillborn! If the people of the thirteen colonies hadn't been so busy with their own problems, if they had persisted and demanded that all the northern lands be ceded to their new federation, there would have been no necessity for this book to be written and the last two hundred years of Canadian/American history would have been even more successful.

Ruled by the fear that Americans would take over, many Canadians have pursued policies of independence based on the goals of wealth-seeking businessmen and local politicians. Their ambitions and loyalties to foreign mother countries have been dressed in patriotic costumes to cover their true motives. Those with connections to European paternalistic nations have always interfered in continental politics for their own benefit, and have managed to get Canadians to overlook one important fact – the only country that could have militarily conquered Canada did not do it, but chose, like the Prodigal Son's father, to patiently let its northern neighbor find its own way home. French and English Canadians have insufficiently appreciated the patient behavior of the fatherly metaphor of the parable. Exactly for whose benefit have the supporters of the British Commonwealth and the French separatists in Quebec acted? So, if Canadians haven't received either prosperity or security from their European parent nations, what have they received for their loyalty? Certainly not liberty.

In the light of the history of the last century, it's hard to understand what advantages have accrued to Canada by so carefully avoiding a merger with the U.S. Britain's effort to keep its colonial hold on Canada through legal (British North American Act), trade (Commonwealth favored partnerships), and unity of language have only delayed the inevitable merger of Canada with its true partner, the U.S. On the French-Canadian side, separatism was promoted at the instigation of De Gaulle, and Pierre Trudeau's policies forced people to speak only French in the provincial government of Quebec, and agitated for a bi-lingual federal government in Ottawa.

Furthermore Canada, as a sop to Quebec, participated in a union of all the international French-speaking nations, which was formed to rival membership in the British Common-wealth. All the efforts of separatists seeking an independent Quebec were put to rest when civil secession was simply disallowed by the government of Canada under Jean Chrétien. The economic benefits of industrialization were balanced with the attraction of cultural independence in Quebec.

Not surprisingly, issues of prosperity for the Quebecois were judged in two referendums to be of greater importance to the people than what would be achieved by seceding and creating a totally sovereign independent Francophone nation. But the decision to stay in Canada was won in the second referendum in 1995 by less than a half percent majority vote, and there are still rumblings of separatism among the citizens of Quebec. The social dissatisfactions of being a French island in an English sea continue to abrade those Canadians with a French heritage. Leaving cultural issues aside, the citizens of the Province of Quebec chose to follow the money that was mainly being churned out by Canadian trade with the United States, and rebated to Quebec via favorable deals made with the Quebecois to entice them to remain in Canada. Naturally the Quebecois, when given the choice, chose the money, not the principles. So much for patriotism of the idealistic kind.

What would our forefathers who wrote the Declaration of Independence think about the progress we have since made? *"We the People, in order to form a more perfect union"*... What have we done to live up to their ideals? Where is that perfect union now? The answer is right before our eyes. We have one continent, our people share similar goals, and we freely cross each other's borders. We should be one country. What stands in the way of unification? It is the flags and fatherland nonsense that has wreaked such havoc on the world since the dawn of mankind. North Americans have taken possession of the concept of their land being the shining city on the hill, but this city is a moral Shangri-La, not an actual physical place. It can move away, as it originally moved here. If we want it to remain here, it is we who must move. We are in the continuum that is life, and we should adjust accordingly. North Americans have the unique opportunity to peacefully create the largest country in the world, the place where the light of Western democracy can be seen from anywhere else in the world. Dare we ignore this opportunity?

CHAPTER FOUR

REPRODUCTION

Y ou probably thought that reproduction was pretty straightforward – just a matter of cause and effect. Well apparently it's not that simple. Sometimes it seems that the population figures have been manufactured. How can one country have one billion, three hundred million people? China does, however, and India is getting close to overtaking them. Why is that important? It is because people are one key to everything having to do with economics, and most everything else too. Just for the sake of comparison the United States has only 312 million people, the population of the member nations of the European Union number 500 million, Canada has a paltry 34 million, and the entire world population in 2011 is estimated to be 7 billion, but is expected to be 10.1 billion by 2100. These figures can't help having portents for the future of our planet.

The second most important factor in the economy of the nations of the world is the relative size of each country. The relationship between the population of a country and its land base tells us the density of the population. The GDP (Gross Domestic Product) is a statistic that tells how successful the people of a nation are in using their land to make money which, of course, relates to their standard of living. When it comes to the land base of a nation and the percentage of earth it occupies, the ten largest countries are as follows: Russia 11.5%, Canada 6.7%, China 6.5%, United States 6.5%, Brazil

5.7%, Australia 5.2%, India 2.3%, Argentina 2.0%, Kazakhstan 1.8% and Algeria 1.6%. A cursory glance at these figures invites speculations from even the most challenged geographer, but this is not a book about geography. It is a book about what the North American people's response to these facts should be.

Land occupies only 29% of the planet's surface, the rest being under water. The actual amount of land on the planet is 148,940,000 sq. kms, or 57.5 million square miles. That sounds like a lot until we begin to divide it by the 10 billion inhabitants of the earth expected to be here by the end of this century. If we assume the population predictions to be correct, we are headed for an arable land shortage that will provoke a land-rush on a scale that will make the pioneers seem like pikers. In China alone they will have to find room for 390 million additional people, and an unusually high percentage of them will be males, thanks to their one child per family policy. It's more likely that the surplus Chinese men with increasingly strengthening military capability will go elsewhere to acquire supplementary land and additional women. The policy that has led to aborting or exporting female babies won't continue. The prospect of the Chinese population explosion spilling over into neighboring Asian lands is seldom considered, but we have the prophetic acquisitive examples of their policies in Tibet, Hong Kong, and Taiwan to warn us.

We can't deny the huge economic progress that China has made in the relatively short time since Mao has been gone. China has rocketed up the GDP charts like a hit song gone platinum. What is the explanation for this? Actually there are several reasons for the success of the Chinese economy. The first, of course, is people power. An indication of this is that more people in China study English than speak it in the United States. The second reason for their phenomenal economic growth is the ability of the centralized government in China to get the population to buy into a single goal, which is to lift its people into 21st century prosperity. It's not a question of com-communism vs. capitalism. It is a question of unity of purpose. Any time more than a billion people begin to march in a single direction, it is impossible not to notice. The leaders in China have recognized that their first job is to raise the GDP so they can have the funds to lift their people out of grinding poverty. China's political philosophers called for modern education programs, hard work, and a heavy dose of materialism. The reason for the success of China's economy is that the Chinese people will sacrifice, at least for a time, their personal goals in order to further national objectives. The Chinese aren't into theoretical ideological political conflicts, they simply want to enrich themselves and their families, and they see having a unified national purpose as the best way to achieve prosperity. In this way the Chinese are the most capitalistic of all the nations.

I have heard it said that China pretty much had to develop the way it has because if a free-wheeling democracy like ours suddenly emerged in Asia it would create chaos on a par with the effect of a fire on a commuter train in rush hour. It is just unthinkable to have a billion three hundred million people running around like chickens with their heads cut off. Some sort of despotism was bound to occur, if only to keep the country together. Whether the current form of government is temporary or permanent, we don't know. We can be certain only that like a huge ship plowing through the ocean, it will take some time to change China's political course, and the changes must be made aboard the ship of state itself. The only thing that North Americans can do to help is to provide the example of a better way of doing things. The Chinese, like all the nations on the earth, will beg, borrow, or steal anything that will bring them greater prosperity. In North America there is nothing that will bring greater prosperity to its citizens and respond to the growing power of China over the next century than a voluntary peaceful merger of Canada and the U.S.

In any proposed North American merger discussions, the Canadians have always suspected the motives of the more populous U.S. as being expansionist. This attitude is parallel to that of the Taiwanese in regard to their being rejoined with China. If Canada and the United States can peacefully merge their nations into one, it would be an example to China and the rest of the world as to how to resolve this type of political problem. Using the North American merger precedent, perhaps China could solve its problems with their independent but similar ethnic peoples. The main reason, however, for combining the interests of the United States and Canada isn't to provide an example of how this can be done. It is to bond together two nations that share a continent and never really should have been separated in the first place. Unification could demonstrate how the *New Patriotism* can modify the arcane ideas of nationalism that serve to divide our peoples, put peace at risk, and limit the economic future of the world. Allegiances to national loyalties that are no longer viable are of benefit to none and dangerous to all.

Population growth has been cited by despots to justify national expansion. Thus Hitler used lebensraum as his excuse for German expansion in Europe. Political idealism is also a favorite tool of tyrants. Marxism attempted to join nations into one dictatorship of the proletariat. It was thought that nations with long histories of mutual enmity could be joined together through idealistic socialism. The idealism, however, quickly gave way to despots who used force to maintain their power. Capitalism finally prevailed, and in most countries power fell into the hands of the wealthy. These pragmatists saw that commerce was the answer to global wealth creation, and they formed international political organizations like the E.U. and the U.N. to promote peaceful trade among the nations of Europe and the world. We are now in the age of prosperity that is governed by international financial organizations such as the BIS, the World Bank, the IMF, and the like. Corporate conglomerates now operate worldwide. The money-men lobby the politicians to get what they want, using all sorts of bribes and corrupt practices to grease the way. Nevertheless we do have a generally improving distribution of wealth among the peoples of Europe and North America, as well as in certain Asian nations.

We now need to ask ourselves if we can we continue to make our citizens wealthy. We have recently seen a recession in a large number of countries of the world. National debt has soared in many nations, and the failure of average people to pay their personal debts has also resulted in bankruptcies on a pervasive scale among the citizens of the developed nations. Apparently people are not willing to wait for prosperity. They want things now, so they borrow the money to pay for things in advance, with the expectation that they will be able to pay back the money in the future.

In the Third World and in the less developed countries the situation is even more extreme. It is obvious that if we want to have a happy world we must have a prosperous world. So, what makes prosperity? Some might say that it is a growing bank account and the accumulation of material things, but underlying the visible materialism there is something else that must be there if we are to prosper. This is optimism. People must feel hopeful that things are coming along. If they have the feeling that their businesses and their national economies are expanding, all is well. If the mood of the people falls into pessimism, we are beaten even before we begin. Investors, speculators, lenders and all people with money, upon finding themselves in a depressed market, will hold off spending their money. This mood of pessimism becomes a self-fulfilling prophecy, and we spin deeper and deeper into depression.

What it usually takes to break this cycle is a massive mood-changing event. Such an event would foster the recognition of the New Patriotism for what it is (wealth creation), and so produce a major vote of confidence in the economic prosperity of the world. The voluntary merging of two democracies like Canada and the United States would be such a game-changing event. The merger would not only give the people of North America a new optimistic outlook, but it would be an example to the rest of the world that there is still reason to hope for a peaceful and more prosperous future under the free market system. If Canada and the United States – two nations that are so close economically – can't manage a merger, how can we expect other nations to make peaceful adaptations to the New Patriotism? When Germany was divided into East and West there were many who believed they could never be reunified. The problem was that the East was poor and the West was wealthy. The wealthy had just recovered from the war, and the people didn't want to have to subsidize the East Germans until they managed to reach parity with West Germany. Naturally the economically-depressed and government-dependent East Germans thought that they should automatically be lifted to prosperity by their wealthy brothers. Nevertheless, in spite of their differences the Germans did the right thing, and with time and sacrifice they made a united Germany into a leading economic power.

We humans have done our favorite thing – we have reproduced, and we continue to build our numbers. Now, like responsible parents, we have to take care of our children, both born and those yet unborn. Are we so short-sighted that we can't see the numbers written on the wall? Are we going to wait until the next megalomaniac despot convinces his tribe that since they have a surplus of people they should use them to conquer and steal the wealth of others? Isn't it possible that we can get behind a plan that recognizes that the New Patriotism must deliver universal, peaceful prosperity? The way to do this is for the U.S. and Canada to demonstrate how a degree of competition can be good, but within a framework of cooperation, it can be great.

CHAPTER FIVE

GETTING IT

The population of Canada is 34 million. The population of the United States is approximately ten times that of Canada, at 312 million. There is only one country in the world that is larger than Canada, and that is the Soviet Union. If the land of the two North American nations were combined, it would be by far the largest country on earth.

Does this piece of information have any intrinsic value in and of itself? Actually, being the largest country in the world has a great deal of political value. Canada is only number thirty-five in population, while the United States is number three. As a destination for immigrants, Canada should be number one, but because so much of the country is located in the far north, it is not as attractive as it might seem at first. In fact it has been said that 95% of the population of Canada lives within two hundred miles of the United States border.

Canada is like a 5,000-mile series of intermittent landing strips dotted from east to west, and that doesn't make for a cohesive country. In other words, Canada is the second largest country in the world, but most of its land is unpopulated or unattractive as a habitat for urban people. On the other hand, it is rich in natural resources. Minerals, oil, lumber, and fresh water abound for people industrious enough to go get them.

As a result of bordering on America, Canada has become the largest trading partner of the U.S. both in terms of exports and imports. Because of this single fact Canada has become an economic power in the world. It sits as a member of the G-8, the eight most industrialized nations, even though it has the smallest population of the eight. I suppose it is an achievement of some sort to have an economy larger than that of Algeria and Morocco, the two countries bracketing Canada in the population standings. It is also surprising that the Philippines, Vietnam, Mexico, and Ethiopia each have nearly triple the population of Canada. Just having more people is no assurance of economic success in this world of ours, but it usually does help. In Canada's case, having had such an economically-aggressive country as the U.S. right next door has drawn it into the American slipstream of monetary success.

Historically a situation like this would have resulted in the larger, more aggressive nation taking over the smaller, lagging one. But, because of its patience and good will, the United States, like so many of its people, has been a permissive and undisciplined parent.

The culture of independence and self-satisfaction in the U.S. has been so strong that by default they have allowed the children to take control of the family. The children have seen this parental good will as weakness and gone their own way, congratulating themselves on their illusory independence, but still using their parent's credit cards and checkbooks to pay for their excesses. Canadians have followed right along with this U.S. philosophy, convinced that freedom equates with national independence.

The forces at work in the world today will not allow this situation to remain static. There are other, not so benevolent patriarchs out there just waiting to take over the disciplining of the unwary prodigal children of the West, whether they are Canadian or American. Of course, as with all simple truths, North Americans will struggle like mad to make themselves seem complex in order not to appear foolish for having missed some pretty obvious truths, namely that Canadian independent democracy has always hung by a thread. In its early years it walked a fine line between English and French hegemony. It won its frail independence from the United States because the American settlers were having similar problems, and were too busy rebelling from these colonial powers to think seriously about the future of their northern neighbors.

Shortsightedness could certainly be seen as a problematic disease when it comes to issues concerning the sovereignty of nations. Those nations whose economies have managed to shuck off the horrible mistakes of their pasts have ended up faring very well in today's world. I offer Germany, Japan, and South Korea as examples of this strange phenomenon. Canada apparently has not suffered the advantages of having had a war with the U.S., so it has tried to go it alone. Its economy hasn't prospered to the same degree as those of the former enemies of the U.S. The explanation for this is that Canada and the United States have been connected inseparably like Siamese twins, but neither nation has been honest enough to acknowledge that they are really related. A formal family reunion is long overdue.

The little brother in this relationship has had tremendous benefits from its big brother, the USA. My apologies to the Canadians who will no doubt wish to give every conceivable reason why Canada should not entertain a merger with the United States, a nation which has often taken advantage of Canada's good will. Nevertheless, whatever confusion and pain is created by such a massive enterprise as merging two countries, it will end up being a great blessing to both nations. The reunification of Germany is a glowing example of the synergies to be had from such a merger. Someday in the future there is little doubt that the reunification of North and South Korea will also rain down blessings upon their citizens. Before launching into the details of the proposed merger, it may help to explore both sides of the issue.

Let's start with Canada.

As I have mentioned before, Canada can't hope to defend itself from a full-scale attack from Russia or China without the aid of the U.S. forces. One hopes that it will never have to. Even if that view prevails, it could be of enormous economic benefit to Canada if they could forego the expenses involved in having to make the dodgy effort to convince the nations of the world that they could actually defend themselves against a large, determined military aggressor. Serious military analysts smile at Canadian efforts to put up a big independent front to support their smoke and mirror approach to defense spending. It is a question whether the constricted parliamentary budget for the Canadian military wouldn't be better off if it were zeroed out altogether as it has been in Costa Rica, another country that benefits from U.S. military preparedness without suffering internal interference.

Recently we have seen several notably futile efforts to assert Canadian military independence. One entailed buying a half-dozen mothballed British diesel submarines at a bargain price. This resulted in enormous expenditures for the Canadian taxpayers with no apparent benefit to their naval operations. The cost of bringing the subs into operational condition has been enormous, and when and if completed, will only result in Canada having an outdated fleet anyway.

Another example of Canadian show-and-tell military policy is their helicopter fleet upgrading policy. For at least eleven years now, haggling has been going on about whether to upgrade the Canadian helicopter fleet, and to what extent to invest in it. The delays caused by a parliament reticent to spend money but desirous of appearing to have a modern military (hopefully without having to spend a lot of money on it), has produced a program that didn't deliver a single new aircraft in ten years. I'm not sure whether any new choppers have been placed on active duty yet or not. It is certain, however, that the first-class, well-trained Canadian Air Force helicopter pilots deserve the best equipment that money can buy if they are to risk their lives flying around in the difficult weather conditions existing in Canada, but they've never been given the unqualified financial support of their parliament. In this case, as in many others, the government of Canada has put parsimony before patriotism. After all the security that the United States has provided Canada, and considering the close military cooperation between the two NATO nations, it is typical of the penurious Ottawa politicians to have ordered the new military equipment from other countries, depriving their best ally of a chance to partially even up the trade imbalance that Canada has created with the United States.

By putting money considerations above military capability and good neighborliness, the Canadian parliament has reduced the financial sacrifices that taxpaying citizens make to support their armed forces. Then the politicians changed the stated mission of the Canadian military and shifted from a purely defensive nationalistic strategy to one of international peace-keeping that supports NATO and U.N. operations. Tactically this effort makes Canadians feel good about themselves and it also makes them look good to the international community of nations while costing taxpayers less, but it is only possible to sustain this policy because Canadian Forces have never really had to protect Canada at home.

No nation would dare attack Canada for fear of provoking United States intervention. To truly protect a country the size of Canada would, if done properly, cost an amount equal to what the Americans spend, which is 4.7% of their GDP for their annual defense budget. This is more than the sparse population of Canada can afford. The U.S. annually spends more on just its military ($700B+) than Canada spends on its entire budget ($550 B). The conclusions to be drawn from these figures are that Canada is wasting whatever money it spends on defense because it can't fund the cost. The operational cooperation between the military forces of Canada and the U.S. are exceedingly close. From a practical point of view, then, shouldn't they be welded into one force?

A full audit of the finances of Canada and the U.S. would reveal that the duplications of functions are so rife that the savings to be had from unification would fund the merger and nearly everything else as well. And this does not account for the synergies, which although not yet known, would be of greater value than what could be saved by removing all the redundancies. The trade statistics between the two countries dwarf even military expenditures in importance. The U.S. annual GDP recently totaled $14.7 trillion, while Canada's was $1.3 trillion. Trade is forever changing, expanding or contracting. At this writing, Canadian exports to the U.S. market are 73% of its GDP, producing a positive trade balance of about $100 billion per year. However, Canada's trade balance with the rest of the world is negative at about $125 billion. A merger of Canadian and U.S. economies would redress a lot of trade imbalances and be of enormous financial aid to both countries.

The military and trade policies of the two similar entities that occupy North America are both costly and wasteful, but the cultural competition that has arisen between the two nations is even more imprudent. While the attempt to separate Canada into Gallic and Anglo-Saxon parts is in many ways inadvisable, the effort to isolate Canada from American culture is even more unfortunate. The Information Age is here and it's not going away, regardless of nationalistic wishful thinking. Electronic communications have enveloped the world, and technology reigns supreme. People like Steve Jobs, Bill Gates, and a host of competent engineers have changed the world forever. We can no longer get lost even if we want to. We get information in our privy or in our pagoda, so it's our duty now to put it to good use.

CHAPTER SIX

STATES VERSUS PROVINCES

The dictionary definitions of these two words tell us a lot about the misapprehension of the differences that are supposed to exist between Americans and Canadians. A state is defined as a country or a nation with its own sovereign, independent government. A province is defined as an administrative region or division of a country. The term *province* goes back to the Romans, and connotes a region that is controlled through an appointed governor. In other words, it is a colonial word. The word *state* derives from the Teutonic word *stadt*, and defines an independent city or territory. The population of a state rules itself from within, and is truly a more democratic idea. The status of a government that rules people as defined by these terms is quite different. In modern times Canada has been moving closer to a statehood system than increased provincialism. Canadians have repatriated their Constitution from Britain, and the Governor General and the Lieutenant Governors are now appointees of the elected local politicians, and no longer Crown appointees. These roles are now ceremonial and titular, and costly to support.

With little difficulty we could relive the heady debates of the Founding Fathers over the principles of confederation. Try as we may we will not succeed in presenting the case for a strong federal government, or the case for States Rights, any better than Hamilton and Jefferson did in their day. We've now had, however, over two hundred years of learning how to adapt to the invalid or negligible differences each country used as reasons to divide the citizens into separate camps. In spite of arguments on both sides, we have discovered compromises that have enabled both Canada and the U.S. to rise to the top echelon of the nations of the world. In order to serve the larger continuum of life, we have found ways to accommodate the smaller divisive issues of party that separate men into camps.

Over time these minor disagreements will become more arcane and minute. Today's North American people are being blended by similarities, and need not be forever divided into isolated individual states, as they are in Europe. Our continent, by virtue of the common interests of the population, is ready and able to be part of a quilt of confederation. Present day North America is composed of fifty states, ten provinces, and several territories, but it is waiting to be stitched together.

The political disparities between states and provinces have had less affect upon the populations of North America than have climate conditions. Demographic studies indicate that there has been, and still continues to be, a great migration of people in the U.S. from North to South. Florida, over the last half century, has become a principal beneficiary of this shift, but it is not the only state to profit from the boom in population. Florida used to be the focus of a real estate scam in which swamp land was sold to suckers from the North who were looking for a cheap way to escape from winter's severity. Who's laughing now? Florida is now the fourth most populous state, enjoying a 300,000 yearly bump in population. At current rates Florida is on course to exceed New York State in population within 15 years. In fact, all the southern states have had significant population expansions. California and Texas, the first and second most populous states, continue to grow. Regardless of whether the reasons for migration is flight from winter weather or birthrate increases, the underlying cause of the fast growth of the states with the warmest winters is the climate. Lesser known statistical studies show that Canadians are making the trek south in huge numbers, too. In the year 2007, for example, Florida was the beneficiary of an 18% increase in Canadian visitors and these "snowbirds" spent $2.8

billion, and the coming years will likely produce even higher numbers. Many Canadians take advantage of recent favorable currency exchange rates and escape the Canadian winter by fleeing to Florida for the season. This annual migration has resulted in many Canadians becoming familiar with life in the U.S. In the event that North America is united, there won't be much of a culture shock for these visitors. Other Canadians, too, are familiar with life in the state that borders the province in which they live. Cross border shopping is a way of life, and depending on the relative value of the American currency to the Canadian dollar, people shop to find bargains.

In the area of professional sports we've already seen and accepted the facts of life. Canadian teams have functioned in cross border leagues for over 60 years. The National Hockey League, Major League Baseball, Major League Soccer, and the National Basketball Association have all benefited from the transcontinental exposure. There are an increasing number of international sporting organizations to which Canada and the U.S. both belong. Whether it is golf, auto-racing, track and field, or equine events, television and the electronic media have brought these competitions into the living rooms of the citizens of both countries. The sportsmen have outdone the politicians in developing a climate in which mergers can be handled with little difficulty. In our free countries people may choose the rules they live by, and they are also free, of course, to place impediments in their own way.

Regionalism in Canada and the U.S. has proven to be a more important economic factor than nationalism. European kings who had never set foot on the land they were dividing between themselves, set many of the borders between the two countries. On the advice of adventurers, soldiers, fur traders, and fishermen having practical knowledge of the physical geography of North America, borders were created that made short term political or economic sense, but which in our day represent unnecessary obstacles to common-sense governance.

In most cases the landscape became the dividing lines between states and provinces. Rivers, lakes, mountains, and seaside features worked their way into treaties that described the vast lands of the new continent. We are now stuck with the results of land policies established by the sovereigns of bygone times. The people of the new world immediately began to set up methods to avoid the ignorant decisions of leaders in faraway places. We built bridges, trading posts, and ferries in an effort to connect people whose interests were not being served by the divisions created by the politicians. Foreign governments set up military posts and customs houses, and imposed tax laws to extract money from the colonists. Pioneers resented these policies and became revolutionaries in response.

Although we no longer pay taxes to foreign potentates, we've let ourselves get stuck with their versions of political and nationalistic ideas that affect how our economies operate. We've failed to take control of our destinies in favor of social and cultural attachments that stand in the way of our progress. The loyalty we show to the nations that our forefathers came from is a kind of tribute being continually paid to undeserving absentee landlords. We have greater needs now that bear on the future of the world. Inevitably the remnants of foreign legal systems have been incorporated into our government's functioning – many of them are still useful to us today so we don't want to get rid of them all without deliberation. Since this is no longer the 16th or 17th century, we should at least divest ourselves of those legal influences that are no longer viable. An example of one of these is the Constitution of Louisiana that is based on the Napoleonic Code. I suppose this is a sop to the French idea of grandeur, but it contains 225,000 words as compared to the U.S. Constitution's 7,000. The Magna Carta has still fewer words, but it has little value now except as an historical document that presupposed democracy to some extent by reducing the "Divine Right of Kings" and sharing royal power with the lords of the land.

So here we are, being governed to a large extent by laws applying to other times and places. The writers of the U.S. Constitution realized that no document can have perfect relevance to every future time, so they provided a method, though not an easy one, whereby the Constitution could be amended as needed. In fact, the document was amended ten times in the first few years after its installation as the law of the land. These ten amendments became the "Bill of Rights," without which the Constitution would not have been sustainable. Since the first ten changes, the Constitution has been successfully amended an additional seventeen times. Most of these changes have dealt with the rights citizens have to be treated equitably under the law. Women and people of different ethnicities were granted the vote, and equal employment opportunities were opened to all. This isn't ancient history. Women only got the vote in 1920, and civil rights were not in the Constitution until the 1950s. The merger of Canada and the United States would offer both countries a wonderful opportunity to refurbish and unify their Constitutions as part of the deal. It would give them the chance to take advantage of the merger to mutually revamp and upgrade their legal systems. Imagine the benefits that could accrue if we had the option to build our new United States of North America from scratch!

The merger would offer the citizens of Canada and the United States the prospect of creating a truly Continental Congress, taking into consideration all that has gone before in government and administrative matters. Every government function could benefit from a new philosophical review, and efficient new automated applications would streamline the democracy practiced in North America. The savings to be had from avoiding clerical redundancies, duplications of effort, and reductions of manual tasks would be huge, to say nothing of all the efficiencies that could be had from making a fresh start. After the end of World War II and the Korean War we saw how advantageous it was for the defeated nations to build their government structures and reprogram their administrative functions anew. Throughout history societies have built upon previous civilizations, using the building materials scavenged from the ruins of preceding generations of peoples that lived there. It has seemed to be a good thing economically to save the cost of building materials by recycling all that could be used again. Archeologists have been kept busy excavating and uncovering one old civilization after another in the same place as they dug deeper and deeper. Some of the great empires of the past were brought low by nature, and sometimes men vying for power over others razed and burned down the edifices and homes of their neighbors in order to take their possessions. Whether it was an earthquake, a volcano, a flood, or the ferocious onslaught of men that caused the destruction, humankind has moved along an unseen violent continuum towards... what? After all that violence, could it have been a peaceful unity that we sought all along?

The nonviolent co-existence of the recent past between the U.S. and Canada is just one step toward the eventual goal of planetary equality for all peoples. We may not like change, but one thing is sure, time is passing and we must adapt. Our chance at making history is either going to include a Golden Age of prosperity, or it will be just another philosophical, political, and religious failure waiting to be uncovered by studious latter-day scientists anxious to explain the political entropy of our bygone civilization. North Americans have a chance now to provide an example of how people can come to agreement with little or no conflict, and through assimilation of diverse peoples reach the next plateau of civilization.

Will we accept this challenge?

CHAPTER SEVEN

THE OBSTACLES

Canadians aren't likely to wake up one day, get out of their beds and say, "Today I'm going to find ways to unify Canada and the U.S." They aren't going to want to trade in the citizenship they know for an unknown future, particularly if they see it as taking the role of a junior partner. The fear of being acquired is present in every organization that is considering merging with a larger one. Nevertheless, a great many corporate mergers have been accomplished by simply making the venture worthwhile for the stockholders. If, after careful consideration people can see the advantages coming from a merger, they will often become enthusiastic supporters of the greater goal. Most people only see the advantages of these deals in terms of their chances for personal enrichment. A few see the big picture more clearly. Those who can't see the larger objective as more important than their personal welfare must be educated and brought on board. In the case of a corporate merger, the stockholders will normally be asked to trade in their stock for an appropriate amount of newly-issued stock in the merged company. They have to be convinced that their shares will appreciate in value if they trade them in, and that the value of their investment will appreciate. In the case of the formation of USNA (The United States of North America), a majority of Canadians need to feel that they are receiving a fair price for their stock (citizenship) and that the future bodes well for the new entity.

The first step will be to establish the reasons *why* this merger should be entertained. Prior to a nationwide plebiscite being held, it must be made clear to the majority of voters that a merger will clearly be beneficial to Canada. No doubt this will require a massive informational campaign to be held in Canada. The period of time leading up to the plebiscite is critical. The response to this issue must be decisive if it is to succeed. It mustn't be allowed to drag on. If the deal is to be consummated, Canadians must be convinced of its efficacy. The will of the majority of people must be expressed clearly. They must accept the principle of combining the two countries into a North American unity as being essential for their mutual benefit. Once there is agreement on this principle, negotiating teams from both countries will have to be appointed to work out the details of the deal. After the negotiators have worked out the particulars, and before submitting it to a Canadian national vote, they will have to explain it to the citizenry in a transparent fashion. In the U.S. the precedents for admitting new states into the Union are well established. It will not require a constitutional amendment. All that is needed is a government proposal that can be approved by a vote of the U.S. Congress. The negotiating teams selected by the Prime Minister of Canada and the President of the U.S. will work out the fine points. The *how* of the deal won't be the source of widespread disagreement, but the *how much* is what counts.

It is peculiar that the least important practical obstacle to unification should turn out to be the largest impediment to the merger, but no doubt it will be nationalism that presents the highest hurdle to be surmounted. In the case of the merger of Canada and the United States, we have already removed the issue of religion by virtue of the policy of separation of government and faith. The divisive force that could have kept us apart is now rendered neutral by our shared policy of freedom of religion. It is no longer a factor. The loyalty issue, however, remains the drug of choice for both nations. What is the key to overcoming this obstacle and establishing a common mission statement? The first lines of the preamble to the U.S. Constitution are a good start. *We the people of North*

America, in order to form a more perfect union, establish justice, insure domestic tranquility, provide for the common defense, promote the general welfare, and secure the blessings of liberty to ourselves and our posterity, do ordain and establish this Constitution for the United States of North America. The central theme of the preamble is that a new set of laws is being installed to guarantee security and prosperity to all citizens. All that is needed is for the people to exchange their loyalty from a smaller to a larger vision.

Attaining wealth is an undeniable universal aspiration of all people. The system that delivers wealth to its constituents is one that will survive. Prosperity in itself will not guarantee a successful pursuit of happiness, but the first step on the road to real contentment must be to dispel poverty. We are all aware of the moral dangers inherent in miserly conduct. We are also conscious of the good that can be done, if in the spirit of philanthropy, the rich assist the poor. In the U.S. and Canada the middle class is continually expanding, and this should be the model that the rest of humanity emulates. The capitalist system is the best answer to the problem of income disparity between citizens within a nation. In a free society that places an equal value on merit and mercy, capitalism will eventually reach a fair balance for all its citizens. When that happens the world will be ready for even greater things, but for the short term we should aspire to stamp out poverty, and North America is destined to lead the way. There is nothing in the world that raises hopes for the future more than a booming economy. The merger of Canada and the United States will surely produce the economic optimism needed to overcome petty political differences.

Benjamin Franklin left us with many words of wisdom, perhaps none so popular as his statement that *Our Constitution is in actual operation; everything appears to promise that it will last; but in this world nothing is certain but death and taxes.* To my mind death and taxes are the children of entropy.

Development is the continuum provided by God to offer us a way to change and improve our situation. We, none of us, know where we are going, but we do know that we shall never get there by staying in one place. The peaceful merger of Canada and the United States offers North Americans a tremendous opportunity to show the world just what can be accomplished by confederation. Our history provides us with examples of how separatism and secession can destroy the good that can be found in unity. The union of the provinces of Ontario, Quebec, New Brunswick, and Nova Scotia in 1867 formed the federation of Canada that was later joined by six other provinces. How much further along with our North American merger would we have been if those provinces had petitioned for statehood rather than dominion? But the Americans were busy putting their federation back together after their Civil War, so the timing was bad. Now the timing is good, and even the most risk-averse politicians should be able to admit that it is better now than ever before. We must not miss the chance to change our future in a positive way.

Increasingly, North Americans are being made to feel that we are despoilers of the planetary environment. Accusatory poorer nations and self-styled, homegrown visionaries are giving vent to envious, hypocritical condemnations of the Western democracies in the United Nations and other international agencies. It is comically ironic how these nations and moralists expect the U.S. to subsidize these organizations in order to accommodate their complaints. We continue to do this to keep a small glimmer of hope for peace alive in the world. What kind of foolishness is this? There are few nations, if any, that given the opportunity would not exchange places in the power structure of the world with North America. Were these nations to take our place in the total hierarchy of economically-successful nations, one must wonder how much unconditional free international aid they would supply to the poorer countries. How many forums for self-criticism would they pay for? Despotic rulers in some parts of the world spend the wealth of their people on palaces, yachts, and personal amusements. Are not these the very same motivators that they accuse capitalism of producing in our wealthy citizens? We must not fall for the rhetoric that ascribes sole proprietorship of the seven deadly sins to America and her Western allies. Let us not forget that envy is also one of these sins. Those citizens of Canada and the U.S. that buy into the guilt trip being laid upon us by slick, envious tyrants should have a closer look at what these nations do, not what their leaders say. Some in the world at large will loudly complain about the proposed merger of Canada and the U.S. We must be strong enough to resist their self-interested dissent, and overcome the obstacles they will attempt to throw in the way of this long-overdue merger.

Perhaps the greatest benefit to be had from the formation of USNA is the chance it offers for both nations to clean up their acts. When forming a new set of rules for governing the new entity, the partners will have to agree on principles. The opportunity to review, upgrade, and improve the operational functions of government can't be overestimated. In order to forge an agreement that will last, the negotiators are going to have to blend their ideas about complex issues into one improved whole that will solve many of the current problems inherent in both governments. For example, the problems the Americans are having over the health care issue could be resolved by fine-tuning the Canadian system to serve the new united nation. A new unified federal tax policy will have to be put in place, which would be a wonderful opportunity to simplify it and make it fairer for the citizens of both countries. Seamlessly blending the militaries of both countries will offer opportunities for removing redundancies and enhancing the capabilities of our joint military, defense, and security forces.

Reducing intercontinental trade regulations will improve our competitive position vis-à-vis the Asians who are presently eating our lunches in the international marketplace.

No obstacle to the merger of Canada and the United States should be allowed to interfere with the formation of a new federation. It will be interesting to see how the debate over the relative efficiencies of the two systems of government can be merged. It will be the first time that such a blending will be attempted. How the political structure of the American constitutional system of checks and balances that maintains the equilibrium of the executive, legislative and judicial branches of government can be compared to and combined with the British system of common law and its two unequal Houses of Parliament, will be the grandest civics project of all time. These two versions of democracy have existed for centuries and have proved their durability and functionality. Combining the two systems, taking the best of each, and melding them into a perfect unity, will result in a truly amazing development in the history of mankind. Political scientists have never had such a chance to ply their trade. No obstacle should stand in the way of this great work.

CHAPTER EIGHT

GLOBALISM

The guiding principle for a great number of people in Canada and the United States has been that they should think globally and act locally. In other words, they should think as citizens of the world, but act as caring members of their communities.

This is good advice as far as it goes. It certainly is beneficial to trade with one's neighbors whenever possible. A tomato grown and sold locally is bound to taste better, and keeping the money in the hands of a neighbor is one way to discourage him from wanting to climb through your window some night in search of money. More and more farmers' markets are springing up in Canada and the United States to facilitate this kind of economics, but when it comes to complex things, or rare ones, it may not be possible to stick to these principles. If you're in the market for uranium, for instance, there are only a few places one can go to get it, and none of them is in a farmers' market. As with anything that is purchased, however, the cost is a primary factor that can't be ignored. If the quality of the tomato you seek happens also to be produced in another country, and because they have cheap labor and the cost is less to you as the purchaser, you will be tempted, and probably will succumb to the urge to save some money. In this case you will be acting globally, but not thinking locally. Does it really matter if your tomato is imported?

Yes, it really does matter. Of course it is only a microcosm of what has happened to the U.S. trade imbalance with the rest of the world. Nearly every economist of note has had things to say about the importance of trade balances in the world economy. It's the favorable trade balance, the difference in the value of imports compared to the exponentially greater worth of exports, which has enabled China to rocket into the position of a world economic powerhouse. Their enormous population has created a source of labor that enables them to manufacture goods more cheaply than elsewhere. Of course it's a lot more complicated than just that. A wag was quoted as saying, "Whenever someone says it's the principle, not the money — it's the money." Whatever the obfuscating explanations made by economists and politicians, we can be sure that acquiring nasty old money is the great motivator at the root of every trading relationship.

That doesn't have to be a bad thing. Everyone in the world understands acquisitiveness, so acknowledging this fact is not difficult. The shame in making money only occurs when it is achieved through dishonesty, immorality, or chicanery. Growing rich by dint of hard work is recognized the world over as a positive thing. While it is still true that Canada and the U.S. are by far the largest trading partners in the world, we should act to strengthen this relationship before China and the other Asian nations divide and surpass us. Every year an increasing amount of trade takes place between the two North American countries. Currently over half a trillion dollars per year of products and services are exchanged between the two nations.

Imagine the improvement in our pricing competitiveness if we were to be united. Remove the delays of customs formalities at the borders, and do away with duties paid to support the absurd paperwork bureaucracies that discourage the economies of the two nations, and see how we flourish! Since our biggest economic weapon is not, nor do we want it to be, huge numbers of people working cheaply, we must concentrate on efficiencies. Nothing would improve North

American economic efficiencies more than a merger between Canada and the United States.

What is shameful is that the nations that accuse us of being greedy, uncaring capitalists are the very same ones that exhibit similar but more extreme behavior. The demagogues who rule these nations enrich themselves while preventing their people from prospering. We can't change this in most cases, but we can offer what help we can, and we can offer a visible alternative to serve as an example of what a free people can accomplish. But we must be strong and unashamed of our success in order to inspire others.

Nothing would serve our cause better than for us to stop feeling guilty for having succeeded. A wise man once advised me to try to live near a rich man because at best I might learn how he became wealthy, and at worst, if I needed something I could more likely borrow it from him than from a poor man. But I say two rich men cooperating can accomplish more than two poor men, so let's get rich together. We can do more for the poor man once we are rich than ever we could by staying poor alongside him. Beyond a certain point, wealth becomes irrelevant. Ask most of our richest citizens what they do with their money and they will tell you that they give it away to the poor, or they invest it in things that will help their fellow citizens. How else can we explain philanthropy? The goal is to end up doing what we love, and often that doesn't cost much.

Socialists claim that capitalist pigs are only interested in enriching themselves. To a certain extent that is true, but meanwhile they are making jobs for others perhaps not so smart or so fortunate as they have been. Jobs are just about all you hear about when there are not enough of them to go around. It is at times like these that the poor can be fired up to protest and blame the rich for their situation. They fail to see the hypocrisy of their words and actions. We have ample opportunity now to make everyone rich. Let's not think that by making the rich poor we are going to create prosperity for all.

Rather, let's give everyone a chance to get rich. We want to raise the common denominator, not lower it. So how do we do that? In the old days if you looked over the fence you could see how the rich man was doing it. These days it is even easier. In North America, if you wish, you can sit at your computer, or watch the television screen and know precisely how fortunes are being made. A long time ago when stamps cost three cents, one scallywag got rich by running an ad in the Personal Columns of the largest newspapers and magazines. The ad read, "The secret of how to get rich. Guaranteed! Send your address and one dollar in cash to -----." Those who sent in the dollar received an envelope a week later with a response, which said, "Work very hard, save every cent you can, spend as little as possible, invest wisely, and don't buy anything you can't afford to pay for in full." That was it. That may sound like a scam, but it is excellent advice.

Living in North America is a foolproof way to get rich. Ask the millions of immigrants who have done it. They came here for that purpose, and none are asking to be returned to the places they came from. Hard-bitten majorities who have been here all along haven't always learned how to get wealthy, but many have learned how to hold others culpable, or blame circumstances for their lack of success. Our free enterprise system seems to them cruel and unfair, so they appeal to the government for handouts, or impatiently borrow money to pay for things they want but can't pay for. Someone once said that if all the money were taken away from us, and we all had to start over again from scratch, the same people who now have the money would end up with it again. Whether that's true or not is impossible to know, but it can be said with certainty that whether you're rich or poor, it's nice to have money.

Annual individual income statistics of nominal GDP in U.S. dollars as published by the IMF, World Bank, and the Central Intelligence Agency of the U.S. in 2010 put the U.S. in 10th to 12th place at $47,000. Canadian statistics trail the U.S.

by a place or two on the list at $46,000. For purposes of rough comparison we find North America being outstripped by such stellar economies as those of Lichtenstein, Luxemburg, Monaco, Switzerland, Norway, Bermuda, Qatar, Netherlands, and the U.A.E. One really gets the idea from the list that small is beautiful when it comes to the annual income of the citizens of these countries. North American median incomes are four times those of Russia which comes in at 57th, ten times those of China in 90th place, and 25 times India at 130th on the list.

It is a temptation to draw all sorts of conclusions from this kind of rough statistical scanning of economic results, but it's really not the past we should be concerned about. We should be looking to the future. If a person is thinking of emigrating to one of the top ten countries he can forget that idea because those countries won't accept permanent immigrants. What does this mean for North America?

There is nothing more annoyingly challenging than when someone pulls up beside your car at a traffic light, guns his engine, and dares you to race, using some obscene words and gestures. That is sort of where we are in the world today. We want peaceful co-existence, but competitive economies are gunning their engines and confronting us. We still think we have the fastest car, but we are being challenged to prove it.

This unavoidable race is upon us and we dare not lose, because the price for losing is ignominious surrender, and possibly a fatal implosion. This is not just a race to see who gets the checkered flag. For the time being at least, it is a global race to the death. Many of us in North America have grown complacent with our successes and have adopted lofty attitudes of political correctness towards our enemies. This is the source of the potentially deadly pressure from within that can cause us to implode. The end of freedom is truly near if this attitude is allowed to give power over us to other nations who see our acts of noblesse oblige as weakness.

One way to keep this global race from producing dire results is to head it off. We want to get such a big lead that nothing but envy is left to the other contestants, but we are running out of time. If we can demonstrate that the practical application of democratic freedom is the surest way to achieve national enrichment, we will have started to construct the destiny for our species that our Creator intended for us. North America is in the best position to bring everyone into the position of universal wealth from which will come the philanthropy that ultimately speaks so clearly about what is the real purpose of being wealthy. If we only succeed in making ourselves comfortable we will have failed in our mission, and we will lose the preferred place in the continuum of life that we were given. The first step is to lift our species out of poverty, insecurity, and ethnic, racial, and religious prejudice.

People working hard at home on their own projects are not the ones who have time to go around the world stirring up trouble. Canada and the United States have possibly one last chance to demonstrate how consolidation can create synergies without the element of conquest being involved. If we don't take this opportunity soon, we may never get it again. We delude ourselves if we think the issues that separate us are too large to overcome. We confuse ourselves if we profess petty national loyalties to be more important than our desire to prosper. We came here to enrich ourselves and to create a society that provides food, homes, and a lifestyle so that our citizens can be as good as they can be, no matter what else they believe, and no matter where they came from. This is what should define true globalism. It is not about building tribal hegemonies or religious theocracies. On the contrary, it is about removing the obstacles that make prosperity for all an unattainable objective. We must get on with doing the really important tasks that everyone longs for.

CHAPTER NINE

MATERIALISM

The thesis that personal, family, religious, and national objectives are subordinate to the search for prosperity by North Americans is correct, but there can be a fatal flaw in the argument if we lengthen the time continuum. The flaw is that if each of us attains his acquisitive pot at the end of the rainbow, we will inevitably be bored stiff. Mankind is a long way from reaching this position, but the vast majority of people do have homes, clothes and food, primitive as some may be. In many places it may not be up to the standard of the average North American, but who would have thought that the earth could handle a population of seven billion people at any level? We do know from seeing how the desire to acquire a few things has affected the people of China. Never in history have so many consumers come into the marketplace all at one time and in one place. We see housing construction occurring on a grand scale in the unheard-of (at least to some of us in the West) cities in the provinces of China. The People's Republic, an communist country has, without admitting it, ironically become the most aggressively capitalistic nation on earth.

There is little doubt that the phenomenal growth of the Chinese GDP that is often over 10% per annum is inspiring other nations in Asia who have watched first Japan, and now China arise from centuries of economic doldrums and make their way to the top of the world's great trading nations. One has only to visit the port cities of China and Malaysia to see how their container shipping harbors have outstripped those of the U.S. and Canada. Are we to suppose that in spite of abysmal pollution problems, the Chinese are going to cut back their industrialization? Hardly. They are expanding at a very fast rate, and they are ramping up for more economic growth. They still have millions of people back in their villages living a subsistence life, just waiting for a chance to move to the cities, get a job, and earn the wherewithal to acquire the toys of the 21st century.

What is our response to this going to be? Apparently we have decided, by not deciding, to sell out to the new economic powerhouse. Canada and the U.S. are selling off bonds and securities to the newly-rich Chinese and Middle Easterners who will soon own our companies and control our government by virtue of holding so much of our commercial paper and debts. Doesn't it ever occur to us how ironical it is that the despots who control the centralized economies of these nations, find the only safe place to put their money is back in our capitalist economy? Most of them were trained to a high level in our universities, and they are well prepared to eat our lunch, to use a popular metaphor. While we spend our time and capital chasing bloodthirsty terrorists in the remote areas of the world, the oil-rich Arabs and the labor-rich Chinese are quietly using our own laws and our economy to serve their own purposes. There are more people in China today learning English than there are native English speakers in the world.
Why? We say it's because English is the commercial language of the world, but for how long will that last? Mandarin, the Chinese written language, is used throughout China, and has united the country. The pictograms used in Mandarin instead of an alphabet provide a better language for understanding mathematics and science. This probably accounts for the fact that so many Asian students in America outperform our kids in math and science, even when they often can barely speak English. A few U.S. high schools now offer Mandarin. How long will it be before North America is a satellite of China?

Suppose that is the way it was meant to be. It is not too far-fetched to think that the mass of human population may soon be the primary force of planetary territorial importance, and national borders and personal land ownership rights are going to slip by the board in the future. Aboriginal people have long held the idea that they belonged to the land and not the other way round. They may well have been right in this belief, and the grasping white man selfishly wrong about calling the land his. When our numbers vastly exceeded theirs, we cynically traded the natives our material goods for their land. When they realized they had sold their land for a mess of potage they protested, and the troops were sent in to march the indigenous people off to isolated camps where they languished and grew weak. This allegory is about to be repeated, only this time it is the ethnic Europeans who are being invaded by more populous diverse groups of foreigners.

Home ownership is the showpiece of American and Canadian materialism. Whether overt or tacit, the principal domestic economic policy of the Western democracies has been home ownership. Our governments have assumed that everyone wants to live in his or her own dwelling, so in order to be popular with their constituencies they set out to facilitate it. Huge financial mechanisms like Fannie Mae and Freddie Mac were set up to arrange things so that nearly anyone could purchase a house. We have seen the results of this failed program in the recessions that were provoked by this policy. Even in countries such as ours, where population density is thinner, the one-family house is not sustainable for every citizen. Group housing is more efficient and the rise of condominiums is an indication of this. In Asia, they may not have had a choice, but neither have they been so foolish as to think that individual family houses can be provided to all their citizens. The high-rise apartment buildings that are springing up everywhere in China have accommodated the move from an agrarian to an industrial economy, producing cities whose names we have never heard of, but which are larger than our largest famous metropolises. We may not want to hear that the adage about a man's home being his castle has been changed to his apartment being his castle, but for most of the people in the world, that is the case.

We have in English a saying which dates back to WWI and states that 50 million Frenchmen can't be wrong. This may be an ironic comment about the French mentality or an observation about the wisdom of the masses, but whichever it is, the fact remains that ten times zero equals zero. The truth is that large numbers of people can be wrong, and often are dead wrong.

People seem to feed off one another. A dumb idea that starts with a few intellectuals can snowball into a great force when despotic politicians take hold of it. Masses of ordinary citizens naively allow themselves to be convinced that they will personally benefit from supporting some foolish ideas that have achieved prominence, and the next thing you know the citizens are being turned into soldiers and marched off to war.

Ironically we are the land-rich aboriginals of today. The agrarian peasants of Asia are trading their old life style in for an urban industrial society that promises an easier, richer life. They have adopted the products of Western technology and are as addicted to them as the "Indians" were to whiskey. The electronic age has completely conquered the traditional life-style of the Asians. A day in Singapore, Kuala Lumpur, or Shanghai is all it takes to see the emergence of a new and confident people that have unquestioningly adopted Western science and technology.

Unfortunately the enormous numbers of inexperienced but over-confident young Asian people haven't lived long enough to see the philosophical downside of the information and technology age. They appear to be satisfied with moving fast even if they don't know where they are going. They have forsaken their cultures and they've used their aptitude for math and science to propel them into an unknown future. They seem prepared to forfeit the development of their human side in a headlong rush towards the modern world of science and its materialistic component. It is not wise to overlook poetry, piety, and mythology. These intelligent young people will one day realize that religion may not be as pagan as is their own scientific reality. At this point they may want to consider the inspiring peace of nature and faith, but they won't find it in the streets of the new cities that their science is building.

Where will they find the peace that passes understanding? They will go to the woods, lakes, and streams. Where will they look to find these things of the soul that are not things at all? They will find, as we already have found, that all the national and personal struggles to get rich, own things, and be an economic powerhouse haven't satisfied their souls. They will have depleted and polluted their lands and disappointed their citizens by substituting materialism for liberty. They will try to copy the North American examples, trying to omit our mistakes. Depending upon how well they have learned the lessons of the policies that led to material acquisitions, they may approach us in peace, but they may also come with envy and aggression. With the big head-start that democracy has had, North America should reach the material saturation point first. Our job will be to anticipate, prepare, and lead the inevitable accounting that will occur when the nations of the world must peacefully halt their race for possessions.

It will be a sad ending for mankind unless we change course. It falls to the North Americans to peacefully relinquish their part in the greedy behavior that has characterized us as the "Ugly Americans." So how do we get from where we are now to the Utopian place where we want to be? The strategy is to be so strong militarily that no nation can expect to conquer us. Meanwhile we must ride the wild horse of capitalism until it dies a natural death. We must provide our citizens with an economy that force-feeds the hunger for material goods till we are like the geese in Strasbourg, and can tolerate no more. But we should refuse to go soft in our comforts, as have all the fallen empires that have preceded ours. Then when the time is right we must voluntarily step back from the brink, repent of our misdeeds, and set a course that honors our Creator and challenges the world to follow in our footsteps.

So what has this rosy attempt at futurism got to do with a book about the unification of North America? Actually it has everything to do with it. We need to make a big splash so that the world can't fail to notice that through democracy and free enterprise we have reached the speed of light in our travels along the economic human continuum. We need to knowingly continue to navigate our path to commercial and individual wealth in such a way as to visually objectify our society, and make it obvious to the world that it is worthy of emulation. We must be careful, however, for pride in our accomplishments can be a worse enemy than the brigandage of nations that want to take away by force what we will have built. There is only one thing that can slake the inbred desire to surrender to the charms of the seven deadly sins, but unfortunately men seem only to learn from hard experience what they must not do. Mankind is at the point now where error seems to be gaining ascendancy. Only through the folly of our excesses can we can learn the infinitely valuable lesson of temperance. Let's hope we are granted enough time to absorb this moral lesson before it's too late even for the peacemakers.

We must be rich before we can give to the poor. This is a lesson that poor people learn quickly. Surely it can't be our task to make ourselves poor so we can be like so many others. Our challenge is to make all people rich enough so they can see the sublime value of giving away their riches, but you have to have wealth before it can be given away. Nothing will accomplish this goal faster than prosperity, and nothing can enhance our prosperity faster than a merger of the continental fortunes of Americans and Canadians.

CHAPTER TEN

WINNING THE LOTTERY

It would be impossible for anyone to foresee all the details involved in working out the merger of two large countries. It would also be impossible to avoid the inconveniences of one kind or another that some citizens of each nation would have to endure in order to receive the benefits that would come from such a combination. Anticipating the problems that would occur is the best way to handle them. Acting speedily is a way to reduce the pain, sort of like tearing a Band-Aid off a child's injury, instead of slowly peeling it off. Minimizing the number and extent of changes that would have to be made is another potentially helpful step in the procedure. Overcoming nostalgia will probably be the most difficult thing to have to live through, because like selling the family home, or laying off a loyal employee, memories and emotions will intrude on the logic of the deed. All that can be said is that if it's the right thing to do, you'll get over it quickly, especially if the rewards are large and immediate. Therefore the benefits of the merger and the plans about how to implement the changes that must take place should be spelled out clearly.

As in any commercial deal between two parties, there is going to be a seller and a buyer. Although in the end there will be one entity, in the beginning of any merger there are two, and they must reach agreement on what is being sold, and how much will be paid. In most cases, and in the case of the formation of USNA, one party will be absorbing the other, so

it's up to the larger country to make it advantageous for the
smaller one. In this case the United States is the purchaser and
Canada is the seller. The continuing benefits in a merger will
accrue to both parties and be augmented by future synergies
that come out of joining the two into one. In order to strike a
deal, the first consideration is for the buyer to do due diligence
and come up with an offer. Since this is a case of nationhood,
the citizens become shareholders and must vote their proxies
to accept or reject the offer. The members of the executive
branches of both countries will have to act as the agents of the
people during the negotiations.

How the negotiators reach the evaluation that generates an
offer is up to them. Certainly issues such as population, assets,
GDP, debts, and laws must be settled upon. Canada and the
United States have a history of negotiating important matters,
and we have managed many times to come to agreements on
free trade, borders, and military alliances. Why not the merger
of our two nations? Both countries have a plethora of lawyers
and accountants that would love to get their teeth into the
terms of such a merger. Presuming that the first issue — the
change of citizenship from Canadian or American to a nation
to be called the United States of North America — is accepted
in theory, the next great issue can be tackled. This issue is the
price to be paid to Canada for making the deal. Whatever the
amount, Canadians will have to decide how to distribute the
proceeds. Because the population of Canada is small when
compared to its enormous land base, the citizens will stand to
get a very sizeable payment as a result. Presumably they will
put a portion of the money in the form of a guaranteed social
insurance plan that will assure a worry-free retirement for all
former Canadian citizens. Probably each province will become
a state and operate independently within the federation as all
the states do now.

Distribution of funds to individual Canadian citizens will
be paid, one assumes, in the new currency. The exchange rate

between American dollars and Canadian dollars has been hovering around parity for some time now, which will help to keep the terms of the deal simple. When the rest of the world hears about the formation of the United States of North America, the worth of the new currency will be valued at an exchange rate greater than the pooled value of present U.S. and Canadian dollars.

Depending on the amount of the increased perceived value of the North American dollar by the world's currency markets, the debts and the trade imbalances of both countries could be significantly reduced in this one stroke. If our money is worth more, the prices of imports will be cheaper for us, and that will address the balance of trade issues that now exist, further enhancing the attractiveness of the merger because it wouldn't depend upon the Chinese to voluntarily devalue their currency, as they have consistently refused to do in spite of the urging of the Canadian and U.S. governments.

Let's put ourselves in the place of the people who are negotiating the merger. What are the things they will consider in determining the offer to be made to Canadians? Will they try to establish the size of the pot and split it evenly between the numbers of citizens of Canada? If they do it that way, will they just take the total amount in trillions of today's dollars and divide the number of citizens into it to get the amount to be paid to each Canadian?

The value of the Canadian economy might be calculated in several ways, but any way you choose to look at it, the value to the citizens of Canada would be a fortune greater than the average Canadian could ever expect to earn for working his entire life. Gaining this level of personal prosperity is the incentive that can overcome all the non-monetary arguments that could be raised to oppose the merger from the Canadian side.

Every Canadian citizen would win the lottery.

Americans may say they're not in the business of making Canadians wealthy, but they must understand that in return they will receive land and resources that would greatly exceed the Louisiana Purchase and the purchase of Alaska combined. The payout to Canadians could also be structured in such a manner that payment is made over a period of time, rather than all at once. The purchase could include elements of future compensation that would serve as prepaid pensions that would remove the stress of retirement funding for Canadians.

Another method that could be explored would be income tax exemptions on future earnings for Canadians. These types of structured terms would stretch out the payment schedule to make the deal more palatable to Americans. Whatever the details of the terms, the synergies that would accrue will be more than sufficient to offset the cost of the merger. In any case both sides would find that the end justified the means.

This discussion is only meant to be a catalyst that gets negotiations started. Each country is well able to bargain for itself in order to reach a mutual settlement.

Almost greater than the economic benefits would be the administrative efficiencies arising from a merger of Canada with the United States. To begin a new nation from scratch using the experience of two great national experiments in democratic government, both in need of revision, presents an opportunity that is just too good to miss. Imagine the benefits of having a chance to voluntarily review and restructure every policy and every department of the national government. It would be the equivalent of having a mulligan on every hole in a PGA championship golf tournament; a chance to do it over again using the latest technology, and taking whichever shot gave the best result.

Never in the history of mankind has an occasion like this ever come about before. To negotiate a peaceful merger between two large governments into one truly modern nation is the wish fulfillment dream of anyone truly interested in politics or economics and their effect on the future of nations. This is a once-in-a-lifetime opportunity, not only because of the benefits to the citizens of both Canada and the United States, but as an example to the world at large. This concept is the best example of what being *too big to fail* really means.

What a marvelous opportunity to revamp and consolidate the tax systems into one improved unified taxing authority! Accountants have told me that at least in the area of corporate taxes, a simplified flat tax is unworkable. Even so, whether we have 60 or 50 states, as far as tax levies and collection of taxes are concerned, it would make little or no difference. The traditionally lower income taxes paid by Americans should appeal to Canadians. A merged Canada and United States would also create an opportunity to revise and unify the social security and retirement systems. The same would be true for the health care systems and the military forces.

Imagine being able to create new government applications similar to the ones available to computer users. Think what could be done in the area of voting. Suppose every citizen had a computer or iPod, and could vote from home or anywhere else he or she happened to be. Every issue would be up for consideration before the nation could receive a true polling. That would be democracy on a scale never before possible.

We might even be able to consider not having a congress or a parliament at all, and have direct representation instead. The pollsters could turn their minds to carefully phrasing the questions before the nation, submitting them to a continental computerized referendum in which every citizen would be required to vote. We would need no more political parties espousing one position or another on behalf of prejudiced constituencies. Through the use of modern-day statistical tabulation methods it might be quite possible to avoid having election polling stations entirely. Needless to say it would be possible to save billions of dollars that are currently spent on antiquated election procedures.

Do away with elections? What a crazy idea! But maybe it isn't so crazy when you take another look at the proceedings at the glorified beauty pageants that are passed off today as nominating conventions. The truth is that the present election systems in both Canada and the United States are costly, inefficient, and undemocratic.

Undemocratic? Sure. Just consider how our candidates are nominated. A slate of political hacks is chosen by a group of people calling themselves a party. These delegates then treat themselves to a party, which they call a convention, in order to select their candidates. How they are selected is much more a question of money, influence, looks, and prejudiced thinking than it is democratic. All that could be done away with, and substituted for a computerized one-person, one-vote system. Every child in the world is being trained to use computers, so why not use those computers and that training to vote on important issues instead of personalities?

Now that we're on this subject, why must we have just one President or Prime Minister? Both Canada and the United States have supreme courts. These courts are composed of nine judges, appointed but not elected, and they consider legal issues. How much more critical is the person in charge of the executive branch of government who appoints them? The President, since his or her responsibilities are much broader, might be expected to have more wisdom than the nine who opine only on legal matters. Is it reasonable to expect one person to have such wisdom? Would such a person, if he or she could be found, be willing to serve? If the requirements of the job of President are so onerous and difficult, why are so many candidates lined up trying to get the job? It almost seems that being willing to do an impossible job should be a disqualifier for any candidate. Why not have nine presidents or a committee of presidents instead of one? We need sages, not egomaniacs, running our government.

All questions like this one, that are basic to our constitutional freedoms, should be openly debated and resolved. When we are considering a merger we should, of course, include a review of our electoral systems. The biggest problem with our current electoral systems is that they don't guarantee that we'll find the good leaders that we so desperately need.

The present electoral systems of Canada and the U.S. are different, but both are inefficient. The merger would require that we have one unified election system, so what better time to entertain the possible improvements that could lead to more efficient methods of selecting our leaders? We may find that we would be better off if we had anonymous presidents, as proposed by author Aidan deVries in his novel, *The Election of Everyman.*

Currently citizens attempt to use their best judgment in evaluating the ability of candidates to solve problems, but we citizens have too many distractions and too little practical information to be able to choose a president successfully. We can too easily be seduced by party affiliations, or by media biases, or by the over-inflated opinion the candidates have of themselves. In fact, the merger may be our only chance to improve this critical weakness in our democratic system.

In the final analysis the economics of the merger are so compelling that we would be foolish not to consider very seriously a United States of North America. Citizens on both sides of the border have listened to their politicians argue and bluster about the need to provide jobs and opportunities for their people. We have heard from some U.S. politicians how this picture would improve if we could develop the mineral resources of the nation in Alaska, the Gulf of Mexico, and the government lands reserved for parkland that comprise 60% of the territory of the United States. These lands, that are being over-protected by legislation could put the nation's economy into an unprecedented expansion mode, or so we're told. If there is any truth to this, how much more of a boom would occur if the resources of Canada were combined with those of the United States?

Disclaimer

I am undecided as to whether this disclaimer should have been put at the front of this book or here at the end. If it had appeared at the beginning and the reader were not sufficiently satisfied with my qualifications, he or she might have decided to toss the book aside. So I asked for the disclaimer to be put at the end, so I could have the satisfaction of knowing that this book might possibly end up being read. As you can see, I have succumbed, like many authors, to the temptation of having my thoughts made available for public consideration.

What is the thesis of this book? It is that the North American continent should have been, since colonial days, one country, and that the land that became Canada should join the United States. For want of a better name the reconstituted land of North America is referred to in this book as the United States of North America (the USNA).

Being a citizen of each country for about forty years qualifies me to claim some knowledge of the subject. As an interested observer and resident I have seen the differences and the similarities of the two countries in a personal way. I have never been elected to public office in either country, and to this point, I haven't been executed for being a traitor either. It's my opinion, based on observation and experience, that Canada and the United States are really one nation that has suffered an undeserved bifurcation. In this book I attempt to show very briefly how this separation occurred, and why it should be reversed. It is not meant to be a complete plan for unification. I only want to point out that underneath it all, the two countries are like great stones in the stream of history; they have both been polished smooth by the flow of the same waters of time. They may appear in the stream to be separate stones, but they are part of the same riverbed.

Aside from just living in both countries for my entire life, I've had a lifelong interest in history, civics, political science, and government, and I've traveled widely. I was that peculiar kid in school who actually liked his classes in these subjects. The first forty years of my life were spent in the United States, and for the last forty years I lived in Canada, specifically in the Eastern province of Nova Scotia.

When I learned that it was possible to be a dual citizen I hastened to take advantage of the opportunity, and even then I saw it as a sign of marvelous things to come. I have voted in every election for which I was qualified to register on both sides of the border. I've started and operated small businesses in both countries. Of my two children, one was born in the U.S., and one in Canada. I have received and paid for medical treatments in both countries.

I have been an employee, an employer, and an investor in both countries. I collect my social security half from Canada and half from the United States, and I file tax returns in both countries. In a word I am an Am/Can, and I know what it means to exist under both the Maple Leaf and the Stars and Stripes. All this doesn't make me a Nobel prize winning economist, or a person who has held high elected office in either country, but by interest and experience I am a citizen with a certain pride and heritage in both countries, and as such I think I'm qualified to express my opinions.

So what you read here is a collection of ideas based upon the intuition, study, and experience of a reasonably educated citizen. I admit that it isn't a scholarly tome or the finely-researched work of an academic, but it isn't meant to be. It represents the collected thoughts of a practical, ordinary citizen who has no agenda other than to see both his countries survive and succeed in a very hostile world. I picture myself as a football player that has made a pretty good return of a kickoff, and now that the ball is on the fifty-yard line, it is up to the remainder of the team to get it the rest of the way to the goal line. My hope is that my team-mates will pick up from where I leave off, and go on to score what would be one of the greatest touchdowns in history. Believe me when I say that I am not a completely idealistic fool. I do see that there are competitors standing in the way, but I still hope that we can get around them and score a touchdown.

There is a commercial for a large banking institution currently being shown on television. The script and storyboard for the advertisement call for a totally random, ordinary individual to be handed a suitcase with a million dollars in it. He is asked to hold on to it until the owner comes back for it. We see the man casually draped over the suitcase, patiently waiting for the owner of the money to return. I suppose the subliminal message is that the bank is honest and will hold on to the depositor's money. I should hope so, otherwise what good would the bank be? Without conscious awareness, the entire population of the world is being asked to trust the banking system, but I confess that I don't trust it at all. I used to work on Wall Street where I found huge snake pit of ever-increasing complexities. Being raised in the Big Apple of international finance has, I confess, made me cynical about the motives at work in the minds of speculators posing as level-headed financial advisors.

A banker friend of mine once admonished me for being cynical. I admonished him back about his being naïve. A person may come down on the side of cynicism or naiveté, but there is a third side to choose from. This side is the frank side. I always aim to take that position. I strive for an absence of artifice in my thinking, so some people may find me too open and blunt in expressing my ideas and true feelings. I try to write my opinions in as appealing a way as I can, but without compromising what I see as candor. This being the case, I do humbly apologize if I have offended anyone by being what I perceive to be frank. I always ask everyone to let me know his or her own opinions of what I say. I promise that I will not be offended if you regard me as naïve, and my banker friend as the cynic.

I'm trying to remove the obstacles in the way of turning a good, long-standing relationship into a marriage that will be a thing of beauty and a joy forever. This is how I see the merger of Canada and the United States. If my genie ever gets out of the bottle and offers me three wishes, you can be sure one of them will be that these two nations will marry and make our continent legitimate.

Some folks may want a pre-nuptial agreement before merging the two families. Fair enough, so let's have one, but let's not delay the wedding any longer than necessary. In time I have no doubt at all that the connubial bliss that follows the marriage will be so great that one day in the not too distant future the pre-nup can be set aflame along with the mortgage that the couple will pay down on their new house.

Quotations regarding the merit of unity as a force for good are rife, and from the time of the Greek philosophers right through to Abraham Lincoln's speech about a house divided being unable to stand, we have been admonished by great men to embrace unity. For these times I particularly like what the Grand Duke Friedrich von Baden had to say on the subject: "Unity makes strength, and since we must be strong, we must also be one."

However, we don't need to be Prussian in our view of government unity. Control of government must still rest in the hands of the democratic people of our nations, but on a federal level we desperately need unity. My inclinations do not lean in the direction of despotism in order to achieve centrality, nor do I counsel my brothers and sisters to fall under the influence of the masses, and so lose focus on the ideals that are most important in life.

So who are my heroes, and to whom do I go for wisdom and advice? I have a crack-of-the-bat theory when it comes to deciding who and what is right. You may wonder what a crack-of-the-bat theory is. When you are attending a baseball game and sitting in the stands, perhaps distracted for a moment by something, then suddenly all your senses go on high alert when you hear the sound of the hardball being met by the solid wood of a bat. You jump up and search for the ball in flight because you know even though you didn't see it, it is going far, perhaps all the way out of the park. It is that way for me when I hear or read something that punctures my usually abstracted consciousness, and makes me focus on an irrepressible truth. Naturally, I receive these moments more frequently from certain authors, thinkers, and saints than from others. I tend to cherish these men and women, and often search their works for crack-of-the-bat thoughts. Sometimes they leave me with apt quotes, but more often with big ideas that need exploring.

Who are my favorite mentors? Usually they are dead, because for some reason we seem to respect posthumous ideas rather more easily than those expressed by the living. My list isn't too long, considering the length of time that history has existed. It includes the following souls, and a few others that I will no doubt leave out unintentionally: Jesus of Nazareth, Erasmus, Benjamin Franklin, Abraham Lincoln, C.S. Lewis, G.K. Chesterton, and Paul Johnson, to name a few who have recently broken through my nearly impenetrable brain. These men will inspire me for as long as I live.

What these particular men have in common is that they have considered the human condition from many sides. As Chesterton says in his book, *The Everlasting Man*, they have come down against the materialist theory that all politics and ethics are an expression of economics. He says that when we think that way we're confusing the necessary conditions of life with the everyday preoccupations of life, and those are quite a different thing. Chesterton says that it is blatantly false to suggest that energies expended to obtain food and housing are the only ones that have motivated humankind. He compares the economics of cows, sheep and goats that, as far as we can see, do not do much other than graze and look for better grazing grounds, and consequently the animals' history would not make very lively reading. They can't make themselves into epic heroes. Men have been Crusaders and explorers. They have left the comfort and safety of their homes, proving that there is something closer to men than livelihood, and that is life itself. Those who think that ethics depend on economics must admit that economics depends on existence.

What a strange irony that I have written so many pages advocating that prosperity and the search for economic success should be the thrust of man's major activity. If you have gleaned only that from my writing, you have missed my point. In the writings of those who have gone before us there was never the possibility of every citizen having the kind of existence that our generation can provide. My point is not that man should only have things that wealth can provide. It is that once having wealth, he can then focus on what is truly important. A hungry man, or for that matter an ambitious one, is not a good candidate for classes in religion or ethics. During our history man has always focused on making poor men moral men. What if no one were poor anymore? Could we not then concentrate on more important matters? My desire is to form such a nation where man's potential for true greatness is relieved of the burdens of security and sustenance, so he can get on with more worthy pursuits.

The existence of a certain consonance between philosophy and science is evident if we look purely at the idea of unification. The most advanced theories in theoretical physics attempt to prove that small physical systems (sub-atomic) as well as enormous physical systems (cosmic) operate under the same physical laws. The latest theory which attempts to make this connection is called String Theory. In political philosophy we also look for a unified theory that will lead us to a solution for the problem of human governance. Isn't it possible that the solution to our political dilemma also lies in unification? And might it not start with the unification of Canada and the United States?

Epilogue

When I started to write this book I thought it might turn out to be a tome. In fact, I saw it developing into several tomes. As I went along I realized that a long book would only contain an encyclopedia of replicated information to support the theme of my thesis, so instead I chose to make it a short book with a few common-sense examples. No doubt I have left out much that could be said, and perhaps included a bit that should have been omitted, but my goal is only to give the ball a push. I have no desire to run downhill alongside the ball. I suspect that, because of old age and the Grim Reaper's tenacity, I will never see the creation of the United States of North America. Whether I see it or not may be of no great importance to the world, although it is of much importance to me. I would really like to have lived to see the engine of human ingenuity that could be built on our continent. Therefore, on a personal level as well as on a common sense level, I would appreciate it if Canadians and Americans would roll up their sleeves and get to work on this unification project.

Everyone whom I've spoken to about this idea likes it, but after a short time they develop a faraway look in their eyes that indicates that they think it is impossible to bring it to fruition, and that I was a dreamer to even propose such a thing. Many people place the impediments to getting anything done at the feet of the politicians. In the case of my proposal I seem to be getting the blame for suggesting that politicians should actually do something original and idealistic. The people of today don't understand how and why self-interested politicians would ever voluntarily begin a program that would eventually shake up their world. We expect so little of our politicians that they can lollygag about in Washington and in

Ottawa with impunity for years. Bismarck is supposed to have said that politics is the art of the possible, but the democratic politicians of today, so fearful of losing their jobs, have made their profession into the sterile, changeless world of the unfeasible. It is no wonder that the American political parties have chosen for their mascots the elephant and the mule. One is stubborn and sterile, and the other that takes a very, very long time to give birth after a calamitously clumsy mating.

So here am I, trained from childhood to be an American optimist. I was taught about the Constitution and the great opportunities for life, liberty and the pursuit of happiness that would accrue to every citizen of our Republic. I'm unprepared for what most people these days call the facts of life. I am particularly unwilling and unable to resign myself and my neighbors to the bleak, self-made drudgery of recessions, depressions, and wars. We deserve better. What went wrong? Somehow we caved in to the Seven Deadly Sins (gluttony, lust, greed, sloth, wrath, envy, and pride). We have come so far along the wrong road that the majority of people are resigned to accept this situation as the norm.

To my mind the situation is fast approaching the critical point. We can either go along with the crowd, or we must break away on our own. As a continent North America has the possibility of creating a better society, but as part of the 160 different squabbling nations, all members of an organization that ironically calls itself the *United* Nations, we have no chance at all when we permit the masses to drag us down. So what do I recommend? I advise that Canada and the United States unite. I advise that we take a time-out in the politics of the world and just concentrate on our continent and its people. We should do this without malice. We should announce to the world that it is our intention to perform a magnificent sociological experiment on behalf of our disheartened people. We should clearly state that we intend to prove by example that the citizens of any nation can have freedom and prosperity by correctly applying the principles of democracy and Judeo-Christian ethics.

In order to weld Canada and the United States into the United States of North America, a referendum must be held. A master plan must be submitted to the citizenry at the time of the plebiscite, and assuming approval, every department and branch of both of the federal governments will be immediately engaged in setting the parameters for merging the functions performed by each agency. The plan will form a temporary administrative department to oversee the installation of a single government that will rule over the continent. When its work is completed this department will dissolve. The plan will provide for the celebration of Unification Day along with Independence Day and Canada Day, and this will be the target day for separatism to end, and unity to begin. For the sake of argument let's say that day is the 1st of July 2020.

Then we should get to work phasing in the new federal government. Every North American should be required to do something to help their new united country. While we are sorting out the details of the merger we must prepare ourselves to defend our new nation from those who might try to take advantage of the situation during the transitional merger period. It must be made clearly manifest that no country or group will have the least chance, through war or diplomacy, to interfere with or impede our progress towards the goal of continental unification.

It is ironic that in order to hold on to our independence we'll have to join together to create a new spirit of patriotism. Universal military training for all citizens without exception should be the first step. This would include a Peace Corps as well as armed forces. Education and training should be of primary importance. The proper use of human resources is of critical importance to the success of the merger. As in every merger, it is obvious that the smaller vessel should blend into the larger one, but every effort should be made to include the things in the Canadian system that are superior to those in the American system.

The objective of unifying the North American continent should always be clearly affixed in our minds. We must let the old die in order to make the new live. Compared to the First Continental Congress, we have an easy job to do. Where they had no model government with developed legal systems to copy, we have two. Democracies have developed along two lines – the parliamentary and the constitutional. In essence they are very similar, but through usage and time they have diverged in details. It will be up to the judges and lawyers of both Canada and the United States to blend these systems into one improved legal system. The principles and documents that are produced in this effort are destined to become the precedents for the future North American justice system. Governance is in need of a complete review, and this is the chance we've been waiting for.

From the perspective of human advancement, the chance to review and improve each and every aspect of the principles and rules of governing ourselves is the single most beneficial thing that will come out of the unification of North America. Every nation with any history at all is always working against the forces of change and progress. The opportunity to start afresh and utilize all we've learned in the past few centuries will prove to be a blessing beyond our ability to visualize at present. We must not miss this occasion. Our first obligation is to our species. It is not to ourselves, or to our nation, or to our race that we owe our primary loyalty, it is to humankind. The concentration on prosperity that I have counseled that we focus on is not an end in itself; it is only the end of the beginning. Substituting prosperity for poverty should be job number one for our new government. Once prosperity for all our citizens is achieved, we can set other objectives. People are always looking for better ways to do things, so we have no worries. Government will always need improving.

Poverty, want, jealousy and envy have made the world the political mess that it is. Removing these obstructions to peace and contentment would change the entire course of humanity. Good will towards men would change the future of mankind from bleak pessimism to bright optimism. Why wouldn't we want that? Along with Independence Day, we celebrate Remembrance Day, so as not to forget the effect that wars have had upon us. Let us now also celebrate Unification Day, the day that unity and peace dawned on us in the form of prosperity for all.

Let us pray to God that human nature doesn't get in the way and, more importantly, that we are not tempted to do anything without his blessing.

Appendix

POPULATION ESTIMATES OF NORTH AMERICA, 2011
An amalgamation of U.S. states and Canadian provinces and territories (in bold letters), ranked from most populated to least populated. Source: Wikipedia (www.wikipedia.org) and Statistics Canada (www.statcan.gc.ca).

California	37,691,912
Texas	25,674,681
New York	19,465,197
Florida	19,057,542
Ontario	**13,373,000**
Illinois	12,869,257
Pennsylvania	12,742,886
Ohio	11,544,951
Michigan	9,876,187
Georgia	9,815,210
No Carolina	9,656,401
New Jersey	8,821,155
Virginia	8,096,604
Quebec	**7,979,700**
Washington	6,830,038
Massachusetts	6,587,536
Indiana	6,516,922
Arizona	6,482,505
Tennessee	6,403,353
Missouri	6,010,688
Maryland	5,828,289
Wisconsin	5,711.767
Minnesota	5,344,861
Colorado	5,116,769
Alabama	4,802,740
So Carolina	4,679,230
Louisiana	4,574,836

British Columbia	**4,573,300**
Kentucky	4,369,356
Oregon	3,871,859
Oklahoma	3,791,508
Alberta	**3,779,400**
Connecticut	3,580,709
Iowa	3,062,309
Mississippi	2,978,512
Arkansas	2,937,979
Kansas	2,871,238
Utah	2,817,222
Nevada	2,723,322
New Mexico	2,082,224
West Virginia	1,855,364
Nebraska	1,842,641
Idaho	1,584,985
Hawaii	1,374,810
Maine	1,328,188
New Hampshire	1,328,188
Manitoba	**1,250,600**
Saskatchewan	**1,057,900**
Rhode Island	1,051,302
Montana	998,199
Nova Scotia	**945,400**
Delaware	907,135
South Dakota	814,180
New Brunswick	**755,500**
Alaska	722,718
North Dakota	683,932
Vermont	626,431
Washington, DC	*617,996*
Wyoming	568,158
Newfoundland	**510,600**
Prince Edward Island	**145,900**
Northwest Territories	**43,700**
Yukon	**34,700**
Nunavut	**33,300**

LAND AREA OF NORTH AMERICA

An amalgamation of U.S. states and Canadian provinces and territories (in bold letters), ranked from largest area to smallest area. Source: Wikipedia (www.wikipedia.org) and Statistics Canada (www.statcan.gc.ca). The measurements are in square kilometers.

Nunavut	**2,093,190**
Alaska	1,717,854
Quebec	**1,542,056**
Northwest Territories	**1,346,106**
Ontario	**1,076,395**
British Columbia	**944,735**
Texas	695,621
Alberta	**661,848**
Saskatchewan	**651,036**
Manitoba	**647,797**
Yukon	**482,443**
California	423,970
Newfoundland, Labrador	**405,212**
Montana	380,838
New Mexico	314,915
Arizona	295,254
Nevada	286,351
Colorado	269,601
Oregon	254,805
Wyoming	253,336
Michigan	250,494
Minnesota	225,171
Utah	219,887
Idaho	216,446
Kansas	213,096
Nebraska	200,345
South Dakota	199,731
Washington	184,665
North Dakota	183,112

Oklahoma	181,035
Missouri	180,533
Florida	170,304
Wisconsin	169,639
Georgia	153,909
Illinois	149,998
Iowa	145,743
New York	141,299
North Carolina	139,389
Arkansas	137,732
Alabama	135,765
Louisiana	134,264
Mississippi	125,434
Pennsylvania	119,283
Ohio	116,096
Virginia	110,785
Tennessee	109,151
Kentucky	104,659
Indiana	94,321
Maine	91,646
South Carolina	82,932
New Brunswick	**72,908**
West Virginia	62,755
Nova Scotia	**55,284**
Maryland	32,133
Hawaii	28,311
Massachusetts	27,336
Vermont	24,901
New Hampshire	24,216
New Jersey	22,588
Connecticut	14,357
Delaware	6,447
Prince Edward Island	**5,660**
Rhode Island	4,002
Washington, DC	*177*